National Park Service
U.S. Department of the Interior

Minute Man National Historical Park
Massachusetts

Minute Man
Alternative Transportation Evaluation

PMIS No. 91491
April 2005

John A. Volpe National Transportation Systems Center
Research and Innovative Technology Administration
U.S. Department of Transportation

REPORT DOCUMENTATION PAGE		Form Approved OMB No. 0704-0188

The public reporting burden for this collection of information is estimated to average 1 hour per response, including the time for reviewing instructions, searching existing data sources, gathering and maintaining the data needed, and completing and reviewing the collection of information. Send comments regarding this burden estimate or any other aspect of this collection of information, including suggestions for reducing the burden, to Department of Defense, Washington Headquarters Services, Directorate for Information Operations and Reports (0704-0188), 1215 Jefferson Davis Highway, Suite 1204, Arlington, VA 22202-4302. Respondents should be aware that notwithstanding any other provision of law, no person shall be subject to any penalty for failing to comply with a collection of information if it does not display a currently valid OMB control number.
PLEASE DO NOT RETURN YOUR FORM TO THE ABOVE ADDRESS.

1. REPORT DATE (DD-MM-YYYY) 29-05-2005	2. REPORT TYPE Final	3. DATES COVERED (From - To) NA

4. TITLE AND SUBTITLE	5a. CONTRACT NUMBER
Minute Man National Historical Park Alternative Transportation Evaluation	NA
	5b. GRANT NUMBER
	NA
	5c. PROGRAM ELEMENT NUMBER
	NA

6. AUTHOR(S)	5d. PROJECT NUMBER
Frances Switkes Katherine Fichter Jordan Karp Jeffrey Bryan	PMIS 91491
	5e. TASK NUMBER
	NPS TIC No. D-96
	5f. WORK UNIT NUMBER
	NA

7. PERFORMING ORGANIZATION NAME(S) AND ADDRESS(ES)	8. PERFORMING ORGANIZATION REPORT NUMBER
John A. Volpe National Transportation Systems Center Research and Innovative Technologies Administration U.S. Department of Transportation 55 Broadway, Cambridge, MA 02142	DOT-VNTSC-NPS-05-06

9. SPONSORING/MONITORING AGENCY NAME(S) AND ADDRESS(ES)	10. SPONSOR/MONITOR'S ACRONYM(S)
National Park Service Alternative Transportation Program 1201 Eye St. NW Washington, DC 20005	WASO/ATP/ and NERO
	11. SPONSOR/MONITOR'S REPORT NUMBER(S)
	(see 5d. and 5e. above)

12. DISTRIBUTION/AVAILABILITY STATEMENT
Public distribution/availability.

13. SUPPLEMENTARY NOTES
This report addresses alternative transportation decision factors as indicated below (Y/N/NA):
(Y) Non-construction options; (Y) park carrying capacity; (Y) life-cycle/ops. & maintenance costs; (Y) cost-effectiveness.

14. ABSTRACT
This study examines issues relevant to the implementation of an alternative transportation system designed to facilitate the movement of visitors throughout the park and, potentially, to sites of historical and recreational interest located outside the boundaries of the park. It provides an initial analysis of existing conditions at Minute Man NHP, and then considers various alternative transportation services (ATS) options in light of these conditions. ATS options include shuttle, tour, pedestrian and bicycle systems that can be implemented or expanded at Minute Man NHP.

15. SUBJECT TERMS
Alternative Transportation Evaluation, Minute Man National Historical Park

16. SECURITY CLASSIFICATION OF:			17. LIMITATION OF ABSTRACT	18. NUMBER OF PAGES	19a. NAME OF RESPONSIBLE PERSON Gary Ritter
a. REPORT	b. ABSTRACT	c. THIS PAGE	NA	56	19b. TELEPHONE NUMBER (Include area code) 617-494-2716, ritter@volpe.dot.gov
None	None	None			

Reset

Standard Form 298 (Rev. 8/98)
Prescribed by ANSI Std. Z39.18

MINUTE MAN NHP
ALTERNATIVE TRANSPORTATION EVALUATION

EXECUTIVE SUMMARY

Introduction

This study examines issues relevant to the implementation of an alternative transportation system designed to facilitate the movement of visitors throughout the park and, potentially, to sites of historical and recreational interest located outside the boundaries of the park. It provides an initial analysis of existing conditions at Minute Man NHP, and then considers various alternative transportation services (ATS) options in light of these conditions. ATS options include shuttle bus, bus tours, pedestrian and bicycle systems that can be implemented or expanded at Minute Man NHP.

The Park and Regional Context

From the analysis of park visitation, the following conclusions can be drawn about the parameters within which an alternative transportation service could be implemented at Minute Man NHP:

- It would have the highest potential ridership during the months of April–October, with a particular peak in the months of June, July, and October and Patriots Day weekend.
- Potential ridership would be higher on weekends.
- At a minimum, alternative transportation service should serve the two visitors centers, the North Bridge, Meriam's Corner, and Hartwell Tavern.
- The possibility of modifying the route or routes offered in order to address seasonal shifts in visitation patterns should be considered.

Also of note is the spike in visitation experienced during the annual observance of Patriots Day, the third Monday in April. The park receives tens of thousands of visitors every year on that weekend, making it a good opportunity to test the benefits of alternative transportation, or even to develop specific alternative transportation services for this day.

Beyond the Park: Existing Alternative Transportation Services

While the Minute Man NHP region is currently served by a number of alternative transportation services, none of them precisely address the need to transport park visitors safely and comfortably in a way that allows them to appreciate Minute Man NHP. The transportation services offered by the MBTA, LEXPRESS, and Hanscom AFB are all designed explicitly for use by commuters, generally operating at hours and on routes attractive to commuters. These services could be used by a park visitor in order to reach the park, but would require the visitor to conform to commuter patterns and would leave the visitor without transportation among the park sites.

Of the five services in the area, the Liberty Ride is the only service aimed at tourists and the only one that emphasizes the colonial and Revolutionary-era history of the area. Its appropriateness as a service for Minute Man NHP has been much enhanced by the expansion of the service into Concord, allowing it to visit some of the most important park sites, including the North Bridge. Its ticket cost and focus on interpretation may limit its attractiveness for some visitors who would otherwise be interested in alternative transportation to and within the park.

Although none of the alternative transportation services currently available in the region fully meet the transportation needs articulated by the park, they do begin to suggest some possibilities for future partnerships and other types of collaborative relationships. The park may want to consider the possibility of partnering with Liberty Ride, or another transportation service like it, to better match the service to the park's goals. The park could also consider working with Hanscom AFB to combine a commuter shuttle with a visitor-oriented service, thereby allowing the same vehicles to be used for different purposes at different times of the day.

Beyond the Park: Partners and Places

Information about the stakeholder attitudes captured during this study point to a number of interesting conclusions about the possibility for a collaborative transportation service in the region of Minute Man NHP:

- Stakeholders are generally supportive, sometimes very much so, of introducing new transportation options to the area of the park. Many stakeholders expressed a willingness to participate in future transportation planning for the area.
- There is clear interest among stakeholders in creating connections between the existing MBTA services in the area—the Commuter Rail stations in Concord and Lincoln and the No. 76 bus in Lexington—and any new transportation service.
- The most attractive service seems to be one that reaches sites in both Lexington and Concord, including sites both within Minute Man NHP and outside its boundaries.
- A successful service is described as one that runs on a regular, reliable, and convenient schedule.
- Stakeholders are generally in agreement that a small, attractive vehicle would be the most appropriate for the area. Several interviewees emphasized that a vehicle with "historical appearance" was less important than one that was handicapped-accessible, climate-controlled, and comfortable for viewing.

The transportation needs of visitors to the area and commuters to the area are fundamentally different in some important ways, particularly with respect to times of travel, places of destination, willingness to wait, and overall flexibility. While this disconnect makes it unlikely that a single transportation service could simultaneously serve both visitors and commuters, possibilities exist for sharing resources between both a commuter-oriented service and a visitor-oriented service.

Alternative Transportation Options

Four possibilities for alternative transportation at Minute Man NHP are considered in this report:

- Interpretive bus tours
- Shuttle bus service
- Pedestrian network
- Bicycle network

All four options are viable at Minute Man NHP, although each has its own advantages and disadvantages. Further study is needed to determine how best each of the systems can be implement at the park.

This table summarizes the relative advantages and disadvantages of each of the ATP options described in this report.

Option	Advantages	Disadvantages
Bus Tours	Excellent interpretive experience Supports visitors with mobility problems Can reduce traffic and parking congestion Supports economic development of local towns Potential partnerships – area towns, Liberty Ride, hotels, chambers of commerce, historic-focused attractions)	Expensive – high capital and operating costs May require user fee Locks visitors into a schedule
Shuttle Bus	Supports visitors with mobility problems Commuter option reduces traffic congestion Can reduce parking congestion Safety – some reduction of short car trips on Route 2A Promotes economic development of local towns Potential partnerships – area towns, LEXPRESS, employment centers, hotels, chambers of commerce, historic-focused attractions)	Expensive – high capital and operating costs May require user fee
Pedestrian Network	Versatile – amenities serve almost all park users Improves visitor access to most areas of park Inexpensive – most of basic elements have low capital cost and no ongoing operational costs Flexible – can be combined with shuttle or other ATS options Potential partnerships – area towns, hiking organizations, local businesses, etc.	Limited application – unrealistic to rely on pedestrian connections between park's units Small audience for trips *to* the park
Bicycle Network	Good combination of visitor convenience and low impact on park Inexpensive – many of basic elements have low capital cost and no ongoing operational costs Potential partnerships – area towns, bike organizations, local businesses, etc.	Improvements to roadways (for bike lanes) are expensive

Next Steps

Based on the information collected for this report and the preliminary findings, there are certain logical next steps to move forward with the development and implementation of additional alternative transportation systems at Minute Man NHP.

Additional Data Collection

NPS staff will need specific data to target its alternative transportation efforts to the needs of the park and its visitors. Empirical observations, visitor surveys, and review of local planning documents can provide the following needed information:

- Visitor use patterns at the park
- Vehicle speed and volume counts on Route 2A
- Commuter transit patterns
- Visitor interest in each of the specific alternative transportation options
- Potential partners' levels of interest and financial participation
- Financial analysis for options with ongoing revenue and operating costs
- Areas of conflict between visitor and commuter uses
- Pedestrian and vehicular uses that pose access, enjoyment, and safety concerns
- Bicycle route analysis including on-road conditions
- Information about existing and previous bike tours at the park

Narrow the Options

Based on the information in this report and additional data collection efforts, park staff will be able to identify the alternative transportation option(s) in which there is the most interest and which they deem the most feasible. After this determination, the chosen option(s) should be developed more thoroughly. This process should be integrated into upcoming GMP and corridor management projects. Additional alternative transportation efforts should focus on the data needed to prepare estimates of anticipated usage, financial plans, and projected impacts on the park, in order to develop more detailed proposals for the specific project(s). A visitor survey can provide much of this information.

MINUTE MAN NATIONAL HISTORICAL PARK
TABLE OF CONTENTS

Introduction	8
Overview	8
Purpose	8
Scope and Structure of the Document	9
The Park and Regional Context	10
Minute Man National Historical Park—History and Setting	10
Identified Transportation Needs/Goals	11
Park Visitation—Overview	12
Park Visitation—Yearly, Monthly, and Daily	13
Nodes of Activity Within the Park—Transportation Characteristics	15
Conclusions	17
Beyond the Park: Existing Alternative Transportation Services	18
MBTA Commuter Rail Service	18
MBTA Bus Service	18
LEXPRESS	19
Liberty Ride Tour	19
Hanscom Air Force Base Commuter Shuttle	20
Conclusions	20
Beyond the Park: Partners and Places	21
Overview	21
Transportation Perspective: Town of Concord	21
Transportation Perspective: Town of Lexington	22
Transportation Perspective: Town of Lincoln	23
Transportation Perspective: Hanscom Air Force Base	23
Transportation Perspective: Massachusetts Port Authority	24
Transportation Perspective: Office Parks and Hotels	24
Conclusions	24
Alternative Transportation Options	26
I. Interpretive Bus Tour Options	26
General Description	26
Geography	26
Audience	27
Timing	27
Interpretation	27
Infrastructure	28
Costs	28
Partners/Connectivity	29
ATS Benefits	29
Additional Evaluation Needed	30
ATP Qualification	30
Sample Tour Itineraries	31
II. Shuttle Bus Service Options	33
General Description	33
Geography	33
Audience	34
Timing	34
Interpretation	35
Infrastructure	35

	Costs	35
	ATS Benefits	36
	Additional Evaluation Needed	37
	ATP Qualification	37
	Sample Shuttle Routes	37
III.	**Pedestrian Options**	**40**
	General Description	40
	Geography	41
	Audience	41
	Timing	41
	Interpretation	42
	Infrastructure	43
	Costs	44
	Partners/Connectivity	45
	ATS Benefits	45
	Additional Evaluation Needed	46
	ATP Qualification	46
IV.	**Bicycle Options**	**46**
	General Description	46
	Geography	46
	Audience	48
	Timing	48
	Interpretation	49
	Infrastructure	49
	Costs	50
	Partners/Connectivity	50
	ATS Benefits	50
	Additional Evaluation Needed	51
	ATP Qualification	51
Comparison of ATS Options		**52**
Next Steps		**53**
	Additional Data Collection	53
	Narrow the Options	53
Conclusion		**53**
Stakeholder Information		**54**

Introduction

This document summarizes the research completed by the Volpe National Transportation Systems Center (the Volpe Center) in its evaluation of alternative transportation opportunities at Minute Man National Historical Park.

Overview

Minute Man NHP is currently considering expanding alternative transportation access to and through the park. For the purposes of this study, alternative transportation is taken to mean any network of transportation facilities and services that provides viable alternatives to the private automobile as a means for viewing and exploring the park. In the case of Minute Man NHP, alternative transportation can provide a number of benefits, including:

- Better connections between the park and the surrounding communities
- Additional means of providing visitor interpretation
- Reduced automobile congestion within the park—both present and future
- Reduced conflict between visitor and commuter traffic
- Reduced conflict between automobile and non-automobile traffic within and near the park
- Reduced parking lot congestion
- Improved access to the park for those who do not drive or own a car

In considering alternative transportation systems, it is important to remember that the goal of Minute Man NHP is to protect the park's natural and cultural resources and to preserve the historic landscapes of the park. Modern roadway engineering techniques and signage may clash with the historic landscape that the park is trying to maintain. Solutions to providing safe park access need to be considerate of the landscape. The park and local communities may consider state and federal Scenic Byways designation in order to preserve these landscapes.

The successful implementation of alternative transportation at Minute Man NHP depends on a variety of factors, including the availability of sufficient funding, the demonstration of an appropriate level of passenger demand, the support of key partners, and, ultimately, a decision by park management and staff that the introduction of a new transportation system would improve the experience of visitors to the park.

Purpose

This study examines issues relevant to the implementation of an alternative transportation system designed to facilitate the movement of visitors throughout the park and, potentially, to sites of historical and recreational interest located outside the boundaries of the park. It provides an initial analysis of existing conditions at Minute Man NHP, and then considers various alternative transportation services (ATS) options in light of these conditions. ATS options discussed include shuttle bus, bus tours, pedestrian and bicycle systems that can be implemented or expanded at Minute Man NHP.

By detailing the existing conditions in the area of the park, particularly as they pertain to the provision of new transportation services, this document serves as a resource not only for this study but also for any future transportation planning at the park. This inventory was developed through observational studies conducted during site-visits; through an analysis of available transportation data, including visitation calculations and parking lot counts; and through a review of earlier planning studies undertaken for the area of Minute Man NHP.

The information collected has been used to help review the transportation alternatives described in this report. Each option is considered in light of its particular requirements and impacts, to understand how different options will affect park visitation, the feasibility of each service, and where partnerships beyond the park are feasible. The section is meant as an initial screening tool that can be used to determine which transportation alternatives should be considered in more detail.

Scope and Structure of the Document

The goal of this document is to identify potential transportation alternatives for visitors to Minute Man NHP. In order to establish an understanding of the transportation-related conditions in the area of Minute Man NHP, the first half of this document analyzes the following topics:

- **Park and regional context**: The history and regional setting of the park, the park's and NPS's alternative transportation systems goals and benefits, and the current levels and patterns of visitation
- **Existing Alternative Transportation Services**: Inventory and descriptions of existing alternative transportation services in the area, including both public transportation options as well as existing tours and shuttle services
- **Partners and Places**: Descriptions of regional partnering opportunities, including a preliminary analysis of the transportation-related needs and resources of each potential partner

The second portion of this document, Alternative Transportation Options, provides a comprehensive analysis of four different alternative transportation options for Minute Man NHP. The description of each alternative is organized in a similar format that addresses critical aspects of the services:

- **General Description**: Overview of the mode and its proposed role at the park
- **Geography**: Areas and types of locations that would be served
- **Audience**: Types of people to whom the option is likely to appeal, based on its services and characteristics
- **Timing**: Variations in service based on seasonality and, potentially, time of day
- **Interpretation**: Opportunities to offer additional information to visitors
- **Infrastructure**: Capital requirements including vehicles, route improvements, wayfinding, and storage and maintenance facilities
- **Costs**: Capital and operating costs, as well as feasible ticket prices where appropriate
- **Partners/Connectivity**: Potential opportunities to engage existing transportation services and other local stakeholders
- **ATS Benefits**: Ways in which the service supports the park's and NPS's goals
- **Additional Evaluation Needed**: Considerations and analysis to be addressed before implementing the service
- **ATP Qualification**: Portions of project that are likely eligible for ATP funds, as not all costs can be covered by the program

The document concludes with a consideration of logical next steps for Minute Man NHP to undertake in the implementation of any alternative transportation service.

The Park and Regional Context

Minute Man National Historical Park—History and Setting

First established as a unit of the National Park Service (NPS) in 1959, Minute Man NHP includes numerous historic roads, fields, sites, structures, trails, and landscapes associated with the colonial period and the American Revolution and it also interprets the 19th century literary heritage. Many of the most important sites of the first hours of the American Revolution are located within the boundaries of the park, including the spot on which Paul Revere was captured during his ride to warn of the coming of the British army, and the North Bridge in Concord, at which the colonists and the British traded fire on April 19, 1775.

The park is located approximately 15 miles from downtown Boston in a fully developed suburban area that combines elements of a traditional agricultural landscape with contemporary commercial and residential uses. The park receives over one million visitors annually. The park's 970 acres are segmented into three non-contiguous units: the Battle Road Unit, the Wayside Unit, and the North Bridge Unit. From end to end, the park spans more than 5 miles running through Lexington, Lincoln and Concord. The park's easternmost boundary is less than 1.5 miles from downtown Lexington, and downtown Concord sits less than one mile from both the Wayside and North Bridge units.

Map 1
Minute Man National Historical Park
Source: National Park Service

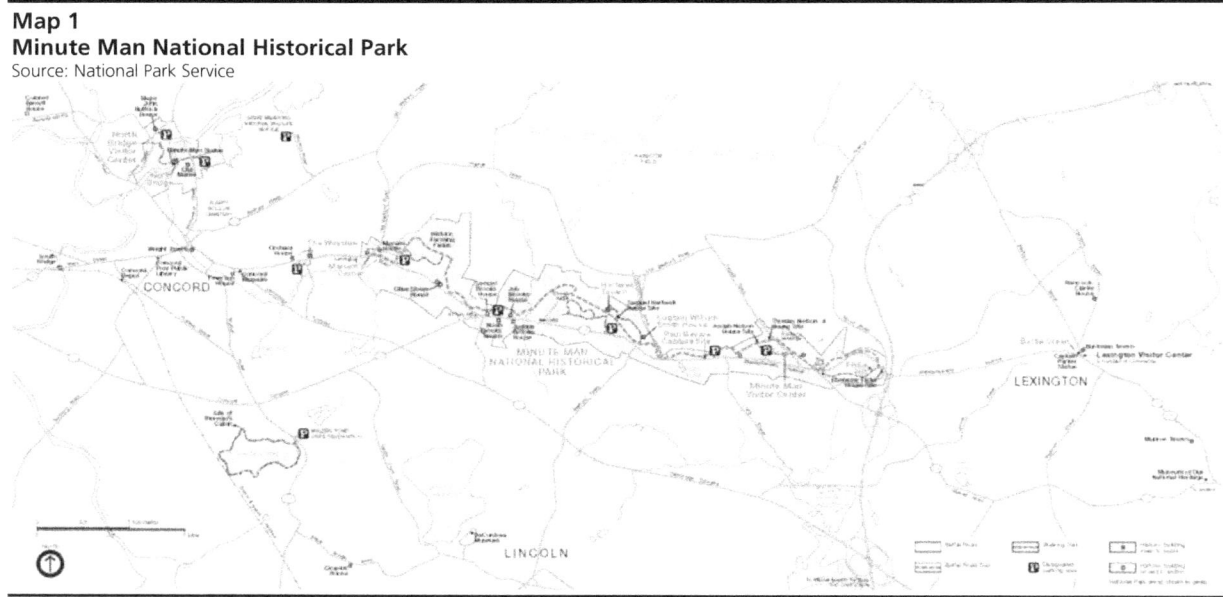

The Battle Road Unit protects the original layout and landscapes along a five-mile portion of the historic Battle Road, the route used by the British to advance to and then retreat from Concord. The Battle Road Trail, a crushed gravel bike and walking trail, runs through the Unit, following the historic road used to alert the colonists of the British's attack where possible, and detouring when the historic road overlaps with modern-day Route 2A. At 5.5 miles in length, the trail connects many of the park's historic sites, making it an important part of the park's alternative transportation network. The Battle Road Unit also includes the Minute Man Visitor Center (one of two visitor centers in the park) and several parking lots that provide convenient access to specific historic features within the unit.

During the 1990s, Minute Man NHP intensified its efforts to preserve and make available to the public the historic structures and landscapes within the Battle Road Unit. This preservation program has continued to the present, with the result that many buildings of the colonial period have been reclaimed by the park and are now restored or are in the process of restoration. As this effort continues, more and more areas of the park—both indoor and outdoor—will be used for interpretation and programming, potentially generating an increase in visitation and an expansion of the typical hours and seasons during which the park is visited. Over time, this will increase the need for better transportation access to the park, with an emphasis on moving large groups of people to and among the sites of the park, sometimes for evening events or events at other atypical times.

As the National Park Service has endeavored to recapture the historic landscape of the Battle Road Unit through the preservation and restoration of historic farming fields, stone walls, and roadways, there has been an increased focus on the character of Route 2A. Route 2A runs through most of the Battle Road Unit and frequently overlaps the historical Battle Road within the park. Route 2A, which is state-owned and classified as an urban minor arterial under Federal Highway Administration's classification system, provides motorized access to various segments of the Battle Road Unit, but also carries substantial local commercial traffic and vehicles traveling through the area, that interfere with park use.

As a part of the reclamation efforts and in anticipation of increasing park visitation, alternative transportation systems are seen as one way to minimize Route 2A's impact on the park and visitor experience. Among other options, the park has considered the possibility of requesting from the Commonwealth of Massachusetts speed restrictions, truck exclusions, traffic calming devices, Scenic Byway designation and historically-appropriate signage and road treatments along Route 2A.

The Wayside Unit, the smallest component of Minute Man NHP, includes the home of the Alcott family and Nathaniel Hawthorne. It is located at the intersection of Hawthorne Road and Lexington Road, between Meriam's Corner and Concord Town Center. Parking is available at a medium-sized lot across Lexington Road from The Wayside.

The North Bridge Unit encompasses the site of the North Bridge, the North Bridge Visitor Center and several historic structures and features. Large parking lots are located adjacent to the North Bridge and the visitor center. Footpaths also connect the two sites, which are less than 0.5 miles apart.

Identified Transportation Needs/Goals

During the initial stages of this project, the Volpe Center Study Team conducted several meetings with the staff and management of Minute Man NHP. Among other topics, these meetings included a discussion of the current transportation issues and needs perceived by park staff. Through these interviews, several primary transportation-related goals were identified and articulated. Figure I connects the park's transportation-related goals and the National ATP goals to the ATS benefits analyzed under each of the alternative transportation options in the later portions of this report. The description of each ATS option includes a review of how that option can support these goals.

Figure 1
Connecting ATS Goals to Analyzed Benefits

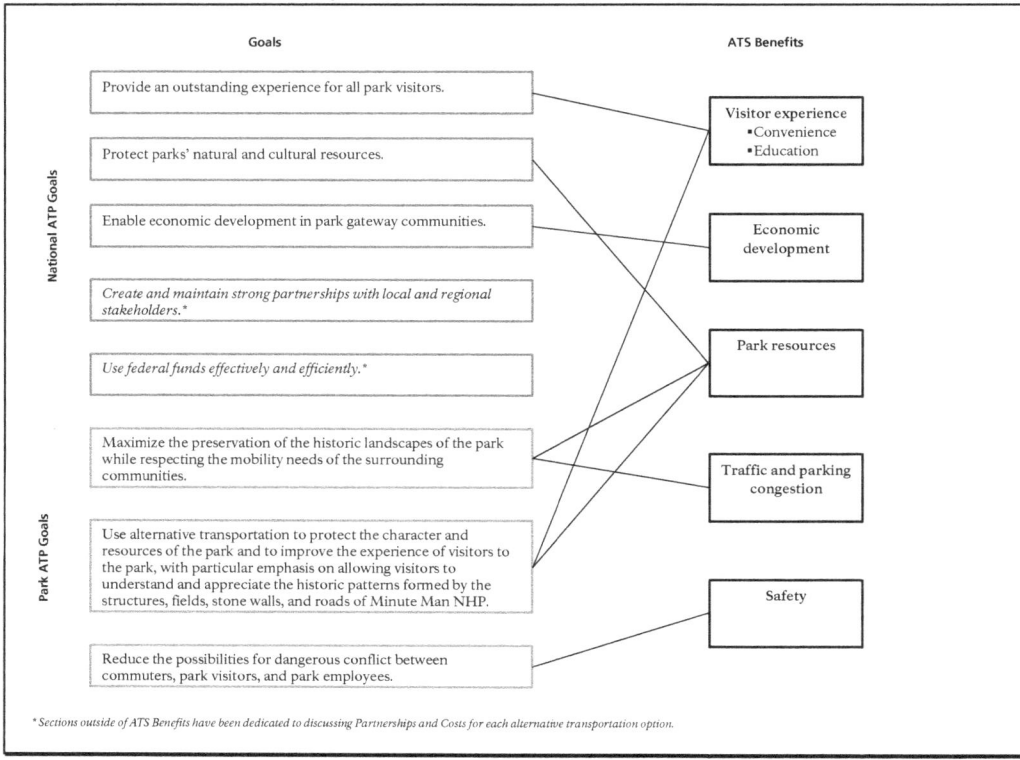

*Sections outside of ATS Benefits have been dedicated to discussing Partnerships and Costs for each alternative transportation option.

Park Visitation—Overview

Understanding park visitation, both levels of visitation and patterns of visitation, is a particularly important element of alternative transportation planning. A comprehensive picture of park visitation makes it possible to estimate (1) the pool of potential users for a hypothetical transportation service, (2) the times of the year and days of the week during which a transportation service would have the greatest chance of finding an audience, and (3) the routes and stops that would be most attractive to potential riders.

In the case of Minute Man NHP, visitation is somewhat complicated to measure, given that the park has multiple sites of visitor interest. The park has visitors who come for the historical and cultural sites, and others who come for the recreational opportunities. A visitor may spend time at only a single site—the North Bridge, for instance—or may spend an entire day exploring the park in its entirety. Furthermore, some park sites are not open throughout the full year, which can alter the annual statistics.

Traffic counts are automatically recorded at several parking lots within the park and reported monthly to the NPS Public Use Statistics Office (PUSO). PUSO then estimates the number of visitors to the park using an established park-specific methodology.[1] The PUSO reports visitation as *total recreational visits*, which are then broken into sub-categories by park site. At Minute Man NHP, these sub-categories include:

---

[1] This methodology can be found at http://www2.nature.nps.gov/stats/.

- North Bridge Visitor Center
- Minute Man Visitor Center
- North Bridge
- Fiske Hill
- The Wayside
- Wood Street
- Sargent's Field
- Meriam's Corner
- Paul Revere Capture Site
- Hartwell Tavern

In addition to the data collected at the sites listed above, *total recreational visits* includes estimates of numbers of bus visitors, special event visitors, and bicycle riders, whose locations are not specifically identified.

The PUSO visitation estimates are important for understanding dispersion patterns throughout the park, but do not provide any information about activity patterns, either recreational or historic. Furthermore, users of the Battle Road Trail are not counted independently of other park visitors, potentially undercounting the use of the Trail. A visitor survey will be needed to develop a better understanding of visitor activity patterns within the park.

Park Visitation—Yearly, Monthly, and Daily

In 2003, annual visitation at Minute Man NHP was tallied at 1.18 million visits. Given climatic variation and other visitation trends, these visits can be assumed to cluster during certain times of the year and certain days of the week. An understanding of the monthly and weekly distribution of visitors is valuable in planning alternative transportation services because such information makes it possible to determine whether a service should run (1) all year and (2) all week, and, if not, to prioritize provision of the service around certain peak periods.

Chart 1 illustrates 2003 visitation data for Minute Man NHP, broken down by park site. As is clear from Chart 1, certain sites within the park receive significantly more visitation than others, particularly the two visitor centers and the North Bridge. From the calculations presented here, it can be deduced that these three sites should be of primary consideration in the development of any future transportation service. Meriam's Corner (10% of visitors) and Hartwell Tavern (8% of visitors) are also of sufficient popularity and historical significance to likely benefit from improved access via alternative transportation services. This analysis is in accord with the information provided by park staff, who identify the North Bridge, Hartwell Tavern, and the visitor centers as the primary nodes of interpretive and other types of activity within the park.

Chart 1
Annual Visitation by Park Site, 2003
Source: National Park Service Public Use Statistics Office

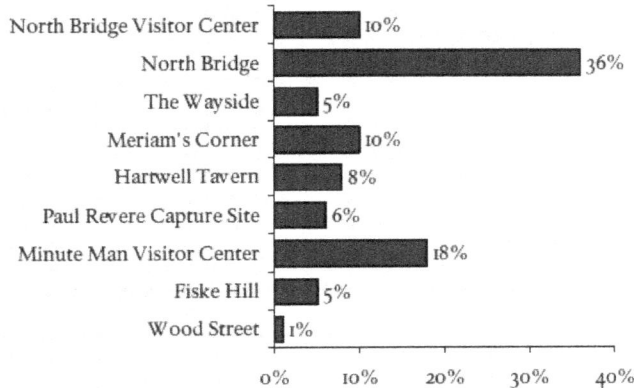

Chart 2 illustrates annual visitation to the park. As would be expected, visitation is higher during the warm-weather months, with a particular peak in the months of May–August. In addition, a spike during October is likely the result of visitors timing their visits to the park to coincide with New England foliage season.

Chart 2
Average Monthly Visitation by Site, 2003
Source: National Park Service Public Use Statistics Office

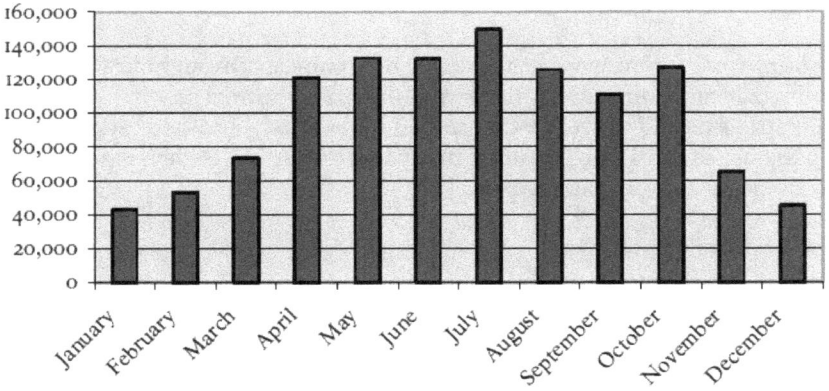

Having established the basic pattern of overall annual visitation to the park, it is important to consider the ways in which visitation fluctuates during the week. Since PUSO estimates are done at the monthly level, a different data source needs to be used to investigate weekly variations. For this purpose, Minute Man NHP made available to the Volpe Center Study Team parking lot counts and visitor counts recorded by NPS employees at five locations on a daily basis[2]: Hartwell Tavern, Minute Man Visitor Center, North Bridge, North Bridge Visitor Center, and The Wayside.

Table 1
Average Weekday Visitation by Primary Park Site, 2003
Source: Minute Man NHP

Day	North Bridge Visitor Center	North Bridge	Minute Man Visitor Center	Hartwell Tavern	Wayside*	Total
Monday	14%	13%	15%	14%	16%	14%
Tuesday	10%	12%	12%	11%	15%	11%
Wednesday	11%	11%	13%	11%		11%
Thursday	11%	15%	14%	12%	15%	13%
Friday	13%	14%	16%	13%	15%	14%
Saturday	20%	19%	16%	19%	20%	20%
Sunday	21%	16%	15%	20%	19%	18%
Avg. Weekend	21%	17%	16%	19%	20%	19%
Avg. Weekday	12%	13%	14%	12%	15%	12%

* Wednesdays at The Wayside were not included, as The Wayside is never open on Wednesdays.

---

[2] Counts are taken only at times during which a Park Ranger is on duty. At Hartwell Tavern and the Wayside, counts are only taken during the peak seasons.

Table 1 presents the distribution of annual visitation throughout the week as identified through the visitor counts taken by park employees. For individual sites, the figures presented include only those days of the year during which the site is open. The *Total* column sums the visitation, by day, from each of the sites and does not differentiate based on whether the site is open year-round or not.

Table 1 demonstrates that the park in general, and some specific park sites in particular, have higher visitation on weekends than on weekdays. At the same time, other park sites, such as the Minute Man Visitor Center, receive visitation that is spread more evenly throughout the week.

The following provides a summary of patterns at each of the sites:

- The North Bridge Visitor Center has strong weekend visitation, with higher peaked visitation on Mondays and Fridays than on other weekdays.
- Visitation at the North Bridge peaks on Saturdays. When compared to a more typical pattern of high weekend/low weekday visitation, the North Bridge has surprisingly low visitation on Sundays and surprisingly high visitation on Thursdays.
- Minute Man Visitor Center has fairly consistent visitation throughout the week, with slightly higher visitation during the period Friday–Monday.
- Visitation at Hartwell Tavern parallels that of the North Bridge Visitor Center, with strong weekend visitation and higher peaked Mondays and Fridays compared to the other weekdays.
- The Wayside has strong weekend visitation, with a steady stream of visitors throughout week.

Nodes of Activity Within the Park—Transportation Characteristics

From the visitation analysis presented here, site visits, and discussions with park staff, the Volpe Center Study Team has developed the following list of *nodes of activity* within the park—sites of concentrated interest and visitation—that should be considered for inclusion in the routes proposed for potential systems of alternative transportation. Selecting from among these possibilities will involve articulating and defining the purpose of an alternative transportation service, its intended audience, and its salient characteristics. Once made, the selections should then be checked against survey and other types of data that provide information about visitor transportation preferences. Also to be considered are those sites outside the park that could be appropriate for inclusion in potential routes, which are described in Partners and Places and within the tour and shuttle options.

The following sites, all located within Minute Man NHP, are described by (1) their transportation-related characteristics, (2) their visitor and interpretive facilities, and (3) the types of visitors expected to be found there.

Fiske Hill & Wood Street

- Two sites, located on Wood Street and Old Massachusetts Avenue
- 11 parking spaces for cars (1 handicapped) at Fiske Hill; 10 parking spaces for cars (1 handicapped) and 1 parking space for a bus at Wood Street
- Drop-off/pick-up potential in parking lots
- Provides access to the Ebenezer Fiske House site
- Entrance to the Battle Road Trail and a walking trail
- No additional facilities
- Users: historic visitors and recreational visitors

Minute Man Visitor Center
- Located on Route 2A
- 95 parking spaces for cars (2 handicapped); 12 parking spaces for buses
- Drop-off/pick-up potential in parking lot
- 4-minute walk from the parking lot to visitor center
- Provides access to (1) Parker's Revenge site, (2) Thomas Nelson, Jr. House site, and (3) Josiah Nelson House site
- Entrance to the Battle Road Trail and a walking trail
- Picnic benches and tables; restrooms within visitor center
- Users: historic visitors and recreational visitors

Paul Revere Capture Site
- Located on Route 2A/Battle Road
- 13 parking spaces for cars (1 handicapped)
- Drop-off/pick-up potential in parking lot
- 50-foot walk from the parking lot to a monument to the capture of Paul Revere and accompanying interpretive signs
- Entrance to the Battle Road Trail
- No additional facilities
- Users: historic visitors and recreational visitors

Hartwell Tavern
- Parking lot located on Route 2A; site located behind the lot
- 33 parking spaces for cars (2 handicapped); 2 parking spaces for buses
- Drop-off/pick-up potential in parking lot
- 3-minute walk from the parking lot to Tavern site
- Provides access to Hartwell Tavern, the Samuel Hartwell House site, and the Captain William Smith House
- Entrance to the Battle Road Trail and the Vernal Pool walking trail
- Picnic benches, restrooms, water fountain, and pay telephone
- Users: historic visitors and recreational visitors

Meriam's Corner
- Parking lot located on Lexington Road; house located at the intersection of Lexington Road and Old Bedford Road (the beginning of the Battle Road Unit)
- 21 parking spaces for cars (1 handicapped)
- Drop-off/pick-up potential in parking lot
- Provides access to historic farming fields and Meriam House, an interpretive structure
- Entrance to the Battle Road Trail
- Restrooms
- Users: historic visitors and recreational visitors

The Wayside
- Parking lot located on southern side of Lexington Road; site located on northern side of Lexington Road (marked crossing area for pedestrians)
- 28 parking spaces for cars (1 handicapped)
- Drop-off/pick-up potential in parking lot[3]
- 2-minute walk from the parking lot to site
- Provides access to The Wayside and Orchard House
- A mini Visitor Center with exhibits is located in the adjacent barn
- Users: historic visitors

---

[3] If the required street-crossing raised concerns, there is a possibility that a transportation service could pull over in front of The Wayside, although there is no obvious shoulder on which to do it.

North Bridge Visitor Center
- Located on Liberty Street
- 44 parking spaces for cars (2 handicapped); 4 spaces for buses[4]
- Drop-off/pick-up potential in parking lot
- Provides access to formal gardens and walking trails
- Restrooms and other facilities within visitor center
- Users: historic visitors and recreational visitors

North Bridge
- Parking lot located on eastern side of Monument Street; site located on western side of Monument Street (marked crossing area for pedestrians)
- 58 parking spaces for cars (2 handicapped); 4 parking spaces for buses
- Drop-off/pick-up potential in parking lot
- 1-minute walk from the parking lot to site
- Provides access to the North Bridge, the 1985 Memorial and interpretive elements around it, the Minute Man statue, and to the Old Manse (not a National Park Service-owned structure)
- Entrance to a walking trail
- Picnic tables and restrooms
- Users: historic visitors and recreational visitors

Conclusions

From the analysis of park visitation, the following conclusions can be drawn about the parameters within which an alternative transportation service could be implemented at Minute Man NHP:

- It would have the highest potential ridership during the months of April–October, with a particular peak in the months of June, July, and October and Patriots Day weekend.
- Potential ridership would be higher on weekends.
- At a minimum, alternative transportation service should serve the two visitors centers, the North Bridge, Meriam's Corner, and Hartwell Tavern.
- The possibility of modifying the route or routes offered in order to address seasonal shifts in visitation patterns should be considered.

Also of note is the spike in visitation experienced during the annual observance of Patriots Day, the third Monday in April. The park receives tens of thousands of visitors every year on that weekend, making it a good opportunity to test the benefits of alternative transportation, or even to develop specific alternative transportation services for this day.

---

[4] The parking spaces here are also used by NPS staff.

Beyond the Park: Existing Alternative Transportation Services

While the transportation network in the vicinity of Minute Man NHP is primarily oriented toward the automobile, there are some facilities for users of public transportation. Three transit services run near or through the park, providing an opportunity to connect the park to existing transit alternatives. Services operated by the MBTA are oriented towards weekday commuters into Boston, although both the bus and commuter rail provide limited weekend service.

In addition, there are a few local shuttle and tourist-oriented services currently operating in the area that may benefit from a partnership with the park.

Connecting Minute Man NHP to the existing alternative transportation infrastructure is seen as important not only for reducing automobile impacts on the park but also for providing access to the large numbers of locals who do not own a car. The City of Boston has the fifth highest percentage nationally of households (35%) that do not own vehicles. Even those who do have a car are familiar with alternative transportation, as 47% of residents use alternative transportation to commute. Boston metropolitan residents have a need for access to natural and cultural resources without a car and the savvy to use alternate modes of transportation to access destinations like Minute Man NHP.

Alternatives included in this report consider not only enhancements within the park, but also connections between the park and existing alternative transportation systems and sites of historical and commercial interest located outside the park boundaries.

MBTA Commuter Rail Service

The MBTA operates daily Commuter Rail service to the Concord Depot, which is located approximately 1 –1.25 miles from the North Bridge, at the western edge of Concord Town Center. The ride is approximately 40 minutes from Boston (North Station) and 30 minutes from north Cambridge (Porter Square). The train has a minimum headway[5] of 40 minutes during peak periods, and off-peak headways ranging from 75 – 120 minutes, which includes weekends.[6]

Approximately 426 people board the Commuter Rail at the Concord Depot on an average weekday. One hundred fifty-six people, on average, use the station on Saturdays, with an average of 112 people boarding on Sundays.[7] There are 86 public parking spaces available at the Concord Depot, and currently no public transportation connects the station with any other site or facilities in the Concord area. A local taxi service provides rides from the Depot starting at $8.00.

From North Station, the price to ride the Commuter Rail to Concord Depot is $5 per ride.

MBTA Bus Service

MBTA bus route No. 76 provides regular service between the Alewife MBTA station in Cambridge and Hanscom Air Field and Lincoln Labs northeast of the park (35 minutes each way). Bus stops located at Old Massachusetts Avenue and Marrett Road and Old Massachusetts Avenue and Wood St. near Fiske Hill are adjacent to walking paths within the park. Additional stops at Hanscom Air Field and Marrett Road and Forbes Road have better infrastructure including bus shelters but do not connect to the park. An NPS shuttle serving Lexington could also share stops with the No. 76 in the Lexington town center.

---

[5] The frequency with which a vehicle operates on a certain route.
[6] Per Autumn 2003 MBTA schedule
[7] November 2003 data from MBTA

The MBTA operates service on the No. 76 every 30 minutes during the peak periods of the morning and afternoon, with service every 60 minutes during off-peak times. The No. 76 runs on weekdays and combines with the No. 62 on Saturdays, following the No. 76 route to Lincoln Laboratory and then continuing to the Department of Veterans Affairs hospital in Bedford. There is no service on the No. 76 bus on Sundays.

Approximately 650 daily trips are taken on the No. 76, with 45% of those trips heading inbound (to Boston) and 55% heading outbound. The majority of trips (90% outbound, 77% inbound) are to and from Alewife, where passengers can connect with other parts of the MBTA system and use a large parking facility. A fair proportion of riders remain on the bus for the segment beyond Route 128, with approximately 100 inbound and 100 outbound trips daily from and to this area.[8]

From Alewife, the price to ride the No. 76 bus is $1.55 per ride.

LEXPRESS

The Town of Lexington operates LEXPRESS, a local bus service that provides transportation on four routes within the boundaries of Lexington. None of the LEXPRESS routes travel within the boundaries of Minute Man NHP, although LEXPRESS route No. 6 travels from Lexington Center west on Route 2A to Paul Revere Road, and then turns around just east of the Route 128 overpass, at the very eastern edge of the park. The LEXPRESS service runs hourly (except for the 11:00am hour) and is primarily used by young students and senior citizens.[9]

The adult fare to ride LEXPRESS is $1.50.

Liberty Ride Tour

In 2002, in an effort to alleviate congestion in Lexington Center while also encouraging patronage of local cultural sites, the Town of Lexington established a tourist-oriented transportation service called Liberty Ride. Liberty Ride is a project of the Town of Lexington's Tourism Committee and is supported by a number of organizations and individuals. Liberty Ride expressed interest in partnering with the park to improve coordination and increase ridership.

The Liberty Ride runs a two-hour historical tour that begins at the National Heritage Museum in Lexington and travels east to west through Minute Man NHP to Concord in order to illustrate the movement of British troops. The tour runs hourly from 10am to 5pm from July through Columbus Day and an adult ticket costs $20 (2004 price). The tour allows visitors to board and alight at over 19 stops along the route and an onboard tour guide recounts the events of April 19, 1775. Passengers are allowed to get on and off as many times as they like during the course of the tour, but they must wait an hour for the next bus in order to rejoin the tour.

Liberty Ride uses a 25-passenger, wheelchair-accessible vehicle, provided by a local transportation

Liberty Ride Stops

- National Heritage Museum
- Buckman and Munroe Taverns
- Lexington Battle Green
- Lexington Visitor Center
- Hancock-Clarke House
- Fiske Hill
- Minute Man NHP Visitor Center
- Paul Revere Capture Site
- Hartwell Tavern
- Meriam's Corner
- The Wayside and Orchard House
- Colonial Inn
- Concord Depot
- Concord Visitor Center
- Concord Museum
- Old Manse
- North Bridge
- North Bridge Visitor Center
- Emerson House
- Sheraton Lexington Inn*
- Holiday Inn Express in Lexington*

* By prior arrangement

---

[8] Autumn 2002 data from MBTA
[9] Based on interviews with LEXPRESS

operator—the same supplier who provides vehicles for LEXPRESS — through a contract with the Town of Lexington.

Average daily ridership on Liberty Ride during the 2003 season, when the route covered Lexington only, was 38 passengers, with the majority of passengers beginning the tour prior to 2:00 p.m. Table 2, below, provides information on the average daily variation in ridership through the season. The operators of Liberty Ride informed the Volpe Center Study Team that the majority of their riders were visitors from outside of the metropolitan Boston area.

Table 2
Liberty Ride Average Daily Ridership, 2003
Source: Liberty Ride

Month	Average Ridership	Adult	Child	Percentage of Seasonal Total
July	47	36	11	30%
August	40	30	10	25%
September	25	23	2	16%
October	44	38	6	29%

Hanscom Air Force Base Commuter Shuttle

In an effort to encourage its employees to commute to work by public transportation, Hanscom AFB has initiated a pilot shuttle service to transport employees between the Commuter Rail station at the Concord Depot and the Air Force Base. The pilot service, which runs once during the morning peak and once during the afternoon peak, has been in place since the autumn of 2003 and will run through the autumn of 2004. At the time of the interview, in February of 2004, the pilot service has so far experienced extremely low ridership: estimates of only a few passengers per ride were given to the Volpe Center Study Team. The service, which is free to its riders, costs approximately $1,000 per week for the Base to operate.

Conclusions

While the Minute Man NHP region is currently served by a number of alternative transportation services, none of them precisely address the need to transport park visitors safely and comfortably in a way that allows them to appreciate Minute Man NHP. The transportation services offered by the MBTA, LEXPRESS, and Hanscom AFB are all designed explicitly for use by commuters, generally operating at hours and on routes attractive to commuters. These services could be used by a park visitor in order to reach the park, but would require the visitor to conform to commuter patterns and would leave the visitor without transportation among the park sites.

Of the five services in the area, the Liberty Ride is the only service aimed at tourists and the only one that emphasizes the colonial and Revolutionary-era history of the area. Its appropriateness as a service for Minute Man NHP has been much enhanced by the expansion of the service into Concord, allowing it to visit some of the most important park sites, including the North Bridge. Its ticket cost and focus on interpretation may limit its attractiveness for some visitors who would otherwise be interested in alternative transportation to and within the park.

Although none of the alternative transportation services currently available in the region fully meet the transportation needs articulated by the park, they do begin to suggest some possibilities for future partnerships and other types of collaborative relationships. The park may want to consider the possibility of partnering with Liberty Ride, or another transportation service like it, to better match the service to the park's goals. The park could also consider working with Hanscom AFB to combine a commuter shuttle with a visitor-oriented service, thereby allowing the same vehicles to be used for different purposes at different times of the day.

Beyond the Park: Partners and Places

Overview

Just as transportation infrastructure and services are part of the existing regional transportation context of Minute Man NHP, so too are the area stakeholders who influence the transportation environment of which the park is a part. Stakeholder participation and partnerships are an important element of any successful alternative transportation system.

The Minute Man NHP region is home to a wide variety of organizations and institutions that are interested in the transportation environment and that could, potentially, partner with Minute Man NHP to support a system of alternative transportation. The interests of these regional stakeholders vary significantly, but all share a desire to improve and expand the transportation options in the area.

Furthermore, there exist a range of sites of interest, outside the boundaries of the park, that could potentially be included as stops in a new alternative transportation tour or shuttle service. This section presents a listing of potential non-NPS sites for consideration, grouped by relevant stakeholders.

In preparation for a more structured and collaborative transportation planning process, the Volpe Center Study Team has begun an outreach process with the following stakeholders, which were identified in conjunction with park staff[10,11]:

- Town of Concord (Planning Department)
- Concord Chamber of Commerce
- Town of Lexington (Planning Department)
- Lexington Chamber of Commerce
- National Heritage Museum
- Liberty Ride
- Town of Lincoln (Planning Department)
- Hanscom Air Force Base
- Massachusetts Port Authority
- Cranberry Hill Associates, Inc.
- Sheraton Lexington Inn

As part of this process, the Volpe Center Study Team has initiated discussion on the following topics with each of the stakeholders:

- What are the transportation needs of your visitors/users/constituents?
- What are the transportation patterns typically followed by your visitors/users/constituents?
- Are the available transportation services able to fill those needs and satisfy those patterns?
- What sites and locations are particularly important for inclusion in a transportation service?
- What characteristics should a new system of alternative transportation have?
- Would you be willing to support the development of a new system of alternative transportation?

Transportation Perspective: Town of Concord

In conversations with the Volpe Center Study Team, representatives of the Town of Concord Planning Department identified a series of transportation challenges currently facing the town, particularly (1) the lack of a public transit connection between the two Commuter Rail stations and the rest of the town, (2) insufficient connections between the recreational facilities in the

---

[10] Minute Man NHP initially approached Walden Pond State Reservation about inclusion in this study. Following discussions, it was determined that Walden Pond State Reservation already receives visitation beyond its current carrying capacity, and so the Walden Pond area has not been included in this analysis.

[11] After the study was completed, Minuteman Regional High School, Lincoln Labs, and businesses along Virginia Road were identified as additional potential stakeholder.

town, including biking and walking trails, (3) insufficient parking in Concord Center, particularly for tour buses, and (4) traffic volumes and speeds that inhibit the ability of visitors to appreciate the historic landscape of the community.

The interviewees were generally supportive of the idea of a park-oriented alternative transportation system, and felt that it would be most useful if it also served destinations outside of the park, particularly the Commuter Rail stations. When asked about the preferred characteristics of a new transportation service, the interviewees identified small vehicles, frequent headways, posted stops, and a continuously cycling service.

Similarly, a representative from the Concord Chamber of Commerce identified the fact that the Concord Commuter Rail stations are not linked to the park or any other destination within the town as a major transportation challenge, particularly for visitors. In particular, the Chamber of Commerce is aware of the need for a service to transport disabled visitors and others for whom walking is infeasible through the park and to other sites in the immediate region. In addition, the Chamber representative listed as transportation challenges (1) lack of public transportation from Boston/Cambridge to Concord, (2) a shortage of parking in Concord Center, (3) insufficient visitor-oriented signage, and (4) a lack of transportation options for recreationalists who want to use the Battle Road Trail but want a transportation service to return them to their starting-point.

The Chamber of Commerce has been supportive of the expansion of the Liberty Ride to Concord, which was done for the 2004 season, and would support an alternative transportation service to serve park visitors and other visitors to Concord. The Chamber representative described an ideal transportation service as one that used a small and attractive vehicle, made regular and reliable stops, and that could serve both visitors and commuters needing transportation between the Commuter Rail stations and the other major sites of the area, including the park.

From the interviews with representatives from the Town of Concord, the following sites were identified for potential inclusion in a new system of alternative transportation:

- Best Western at Colonial Concord
- Colonial Inn
- Concord Commuter Rail stations (Concord Depot and West Concord)
- Concord Museum

Transportation Perspective: Town of Lexington

The Town of Lexington, in conjunction with private supporters, has been the driving force behind the establishment of Liberty Ride. An interviewee from the Town of Lexington Planning Department expressed his belief that an expanded tourism-oriented transportation service like Liberty Ride could be of great value to the Minute Man NHP region, particularly if it were able to serve a constellation of sites within both Lexington and Concord. The interviewee emphasized that such a service must be reliable and convenient for visitors, however, and must provide an attractive alternative to the private automobile. The interviewee also argued that municipal and institutional support for such a service is a key component of its success and that transportation services generally require a dedicated source of funding.

Like the Town of Lexington, the Lexington Chamber of Commerce has been heavily involved with the development and promotion of Liberty Ride. The representative of the Chamber expressed her belief that Liberty Ride serves an important need for visitors to be able to see the sites of Lexington without a private car, and that visitors will be well-served by an expansion of the service into Concord. In general, the Chamber interviewee feels that a transportation service providing interpretation, on a small and comfortable vehicle, with reliable service and headways of no more than 30 minutes, would be a valuable addition to the town and should be supported.

A representative of the Lexington-based National Heritage Museum—located at the intersection of Route 2A and Massachusetts Avenue—was also very much in support of a tourist-oriented transportation service that could provide transit both to the park and to other sites in Lexington and Concord, including the Commuter Rail stations. In addition, the No. 76 bus from Alewife travels by the Museum without currently stopping there, suggesting the possibility of future connectivity between the MBTA and an alternative transportation service with a hub at the Museum.[12] The Museum representative emphasized that a transportation service linking the Battle Road Unit with other regional locations and landscapes of the colonial and Revolutionary period could offer passengers a tangible way to visualize the events of April 19, 1775.

From the interviews with representatives from the Town of Lexington, the following sites were identified for potential inclusion in a new system of alternative transportation:

- Alewife intermodal MBTA station
- Historic sites managed by the Lexington Historical Society
- Lexington Battle Green
- National Heritage Museum

Transportation Perspective: Town of Lincoln

The representative of the Town of Lincoln Planning Department stated that while park-oriented traffic does not have a major impact on Lincoln, he would be in favor of introducing new transportation options in the region. In particular, he feels that the Town of Lincoln has a need to create better connectivity between the Lincoln Commuter Rail station, the commercial center of Lincoln, and residential neighborhoods in the area of the park. In addition, the interviewee identified the DeCordova Museum and Sculpture Park, in south Lincoln, as a site of potential interest for visitors, as well as Drumlin Farm Wildlife Sanctuary, a facility of the Massachusetts Audubon Society. Lastly, the interviewee emphasized the need for better transportation connections to Battle Road Farm, a mixed-income housing development located in north Lincoln.

From the interview with the representative from the Town of Lincoln, the following sites were identified for potential inclusion in a new system of alternative transportation:

- Battle Road Farm
- DeCordova Museum and Sculpture Park
- Drumlin Farm Wildlife Sanctuary
- Lincoln Commuter Rail Station

Transportation Perspective: Hanscom Air Force Base

As described, Hanscom AFB is currently operating a pilot shuttle service to transport employees between the Base and the Concord Depot. This service has so far achieved minimal ridership and is unlikely to substantially influence the transportation patterns of Base employees, the vast majority of who commute to and from work by private automobile. Although Base administrators have considered other means to encourage the use alternative transportation, the typical transportation patterns of Base employees—traveling at off-peak hours, traveling from diverse locations, and using automobiles to travel within the Base as part of the work-day—all make it difficult to develop a transportation service that would be attractive to a sizable segment of the Base population. Nevertheless, the Base representative voiced support for the idea of a transportation service designed to transport park visitors, particularly one that included other sites of interest in Concord and Lexington. The Base representative also expressed interest in the possibility of sharing the cost and responsibility of the Hanscom AFB shuttle service—should it

---

[12] Liberty Ride currently uses the Museum as its eastern terminus.

continue beyond its pilot phase—with the park, perhaps by combining a visitor-oriented service with the Base-operated shuttle.

From the interview with representative from the U.S. Air Force, the following sites were identified for potential inclusion in a new system of alternative transportation:

- Commuter Rail stations

Transportation Perspective: Massachusetts Port Authority

From conversations with a representative of the Massachusetts Port Authority (Massport)—the public agency responsible for the civilian airport at Hanscom Field—it seems that travelers to the airport follow similar, although not identical, transportation patterns to those travelers to Hanscom AFB. The vast majority travel there by automobile, often at off-peak times, with few to none using regional public transit services. Unlike travelers to Hanscom AFB, approximately 50% of the passengers traveling to the civilian airport come from one of the communities neighboring Hanscom Field. The Massport representative felt it to be unlikely that an alternative transportation service would be appealing to the users of the civilian airport, although there remains a possibility that an appropriately designed service could be used by airport employees.

Transportation Perspective: Office Parks and Hotels

The Lincoln North office park, managed by Cranberry Hill Associates, Inc. and located just beyond the eastern edge of the park, houses approximately 200 employees, only one of whom is reported to use public transit services to reach the office. From interviews with the owner/developer of Lincoln North, it is clear that the bulk of the tenants of the building are not likely to use any sort of alternative transportation service and that the possibility of successfully combining a transportation service intended for park visitors with one for commuters to Lincoln North is very low.

The Sheraton Lexington Inn, located on the eastern side of Route 128, is an active participant in the Liberty Ride service—as both a contributor and an optional stop on the tour route—and would be supportive of an expanded system of alternative transportation for the area. Although the majority of the individuals who stay at the Inn are weekday business travelers, groups of weekend guests often express interest in having a convenient way to see the historic and cultural sites of the area without a car. More generally, the Inn would support any effort to provide more transportation options in the region, as the lack of transportation alternatives is believed to discourage some customers from using the Inn. At present, the Inn offers its own shuttle service for extended-stay guests who are in need of a way to travel to the commercial and retail areas in the region. The shuttle will also transport guests to the MBTA station at Alewife.

Conclusions

Although the stakeholder attitudes captured here are based on preliminary conversations only, they point to a number of interesting conclusions about the possibility for a collaborative transportation service in the region of Minute Man NHP:

- Stakeholders are generally supportive, sometimes very much so, of introducing new transportation options to the area of the park. Many stakeholders expressed a willingness to participate in future transportation planning for the area.
- There is clear interest among stakeholders in creating connections between the existing MBTA services in the area—the Commuter Rail stations in Concord and Lincoln and the No. 76 bus in Lexington—and any new transportation service.
- The most attractive service seems to be one that reaches sites in both Lexington and Concord, including sites both within Minute Man NHP and outside its boundaries.

- A successful service is described as one that runs on a regular, reliable, and convenient schedule.
- Stakeholders are generally in agreement that a small, attractive vehicle would be the most appropriate for the area. Several interviewees emphasized that a vehicle with "historical appearance" was less important than one that was handicapped-accessible, climate-controlled, and comfortable for viewing.

The transportation needs of visitors to the area and commuters to the area are fundamentally different in some important ways, particularly with respect to times of travel, places of destination, willingness to wait, and overall flexibility. While this disconnect makes it unlikely that a single transportation service could simultaneously serve both visitors and commuters, possibilities exist for sharing resources between both a commuter-oriented service and a visitor-oriented service.

Alternative Transportation Options

This section provides an initial analysis of how four alternative transportation services can be initiated or expanded at Minute Man NHP:

- Interpretive bus tours
- Shuttle bus service
- Pedestrian network
- Bicycle network

The information about existing conditions presented in the first sections of this report has been used to help shape the transportation alternatives described below, to understand how different options will affect park visitation, and where partnerships beyond the park are feasible. These descriptions discuss the requirements and impacts of different categories of transportation improvements and are meant to be an initial screening tool that can be used to determine which transportation alternatives should be considered in more detail.

I.   Interpretive Bus Tour Options

General Description

An interpretive bus tour provides a structured combination of transportation and information for visitors. Tour participants are picked up in a specific location and driven on a fixed route through the area. A tour's primary focus is on local sites of interest, about which historical and cultural information is presented both en route and at selected sites. The tour can span the entire park as well as any additional non-NPS locations desired, with stops at selected sites. The tour is structured so that passengers can remain with the same tour guide and vehicle throughout the tour (possibly without ever exiting the vehicle) if they prefer, or can use the service on a "shuttle" basis similar to the existing Liberty Ride tour whereby they can leave the tour vehicle and get on the next one that arrives.

Bus tours reduce congestion both on park roads and in parking lots by eliminating the need for visitors to drive from site to site. By locating tour starting points outside of the park, the service can even eliminate the need for visitors to bring their cars into the park at all.

Geography

Three general categories of sites should be considered for inclusion in tour itineraries:

- Minute Man NHP sites
- Historical and cultural sites in Concord
- Historical and cultural sites in Lexington

A tour can include any combination of sites from these categories. The two most likely options are (1) a "Minute Man NHP-only" option, which travels only to sites within the park; and (2) a "Concord/Lexington area" option, which adds other local sites of interest to the itinerary.

Both of these options have advantages and drawbacks. Adding sites outside of the park increases the tour route distance and cycle time; this increases operating costs and reduces the number of tours in a given day. The inclusion of non-NPS sites offers the benefit of partnership opportunities with local towns, and may attract more riders by casting a "wider net" for ridership. The tour route should also be determined by visitors' willingness to take tours of varying durations; many visitors may not be willing to commit to a longer tour, although the longer route presents a more complete story of the pre-revolutionary events in the area. The two sample tour routes on pages 31-33 illustrate the trade-offs of longer and shorter routes.

Tour start/finish locations should be selected carefully. Adequate parking is the primary consideration, since cars will remain parked for the duration of the tour. Ideally, tours start outside of the park, so visitors do not need to drive on Route 2A or in the park. Nearby partners who do not use their parking lots during summers or weekends may be willing to serve as a starting point for a tour. Prospective sites within Minute Man NHP that can be used as tour starting points are the two visitor centers, since they have the largest parking lots. Even these lots, however, have insufficient capacity: tour participants' cars remain parked in place for longer periods, occupying a single space that would otherwise be used by multiple consecutive self-driven visitors during brief stops at that location; this causes a parking shortage for self-driven visitors.

Since the tour start/finish locations are heavily dependent on parking capacity and likely sites are not near local transit services, it may be impractical to target transit users for participation in the tours. The increased cycle time of a tour also makes it difficult to coordinate tour vehicle timing with transit vehicle arrivals/departures. While one potential tour route presented in this section considers a stop at the Concord Depot, passengers starting the tour from this location would hear the "Minute Man story" out of sequence.

Audience

The primary audience for an interpretive tour service is history-oriented visitors interested in learning about Minute Man NHP and nearby sites. Tours offer them a convenient, structured means of visiting the significant sites while receiving additional information that supplements the on-site interpretive displays. Many people, particularly those unfamiliar with the area, appreciate the opportunity to be transported from site to site without having to navigate by themselves and to find parking at each stop.

Trips offered by a tour service appeal less to commuters and local travelers, who are more concerned with low cost and efficient speed for their transportation.

Timing

Tours should be offered several times a day, especially on weekends and holidays during the peak season of April through October, and on Patriots Day weekend in April.

Typically, visitors tolerate longer intervals between the departure times of tours than between shuttle services, since the tours themselves are a "destination" event around which visitors plan their schedule. Tour headways, or the amount of time between tours, should not exceed 60 minutes to attract sufficient riders, although shorter headways provide more flexibility for visitors. The frequency of tours will be limited by the number of vehicles available for use and the length of the tour route.

In comparison to the shuttle bus option discussed in the next section, interpretive tours are generally a longer experience because they involve interpretive presentations at most or all stops. Tour participants are generally willing to undertake a longer journey because they are receiving more information than shuttle riders. A visitor survey would be useful to determine the appropriate length of a service.

Interpretation

The tour should include on-vehicle interpretation, ideally provided by an NPS staff person other than the driver, who can narrate and answer passengers' questions. Alternate media can also be used for special topics, or during the off-peak season to reduce staffing requirements. Both options supplement the existing interpretive services in the park without requiring additional interpretive infrastructure to be developed within the park landscape.

Infrastructure

Interpretive tour service requires four principal types of infrastructure: vehicles, stops/signposting, staffing, and a storage/maintenance facility. In the case of a concession agreement between the NPS and a private contractor, costs for vehicles, staffing and storage facilities could be handled by the concessionaire. If the park chooses to contract for only operation and maintenance of a service, the park would need to purchase vehicles and build and maintain a storage and basic maintenance facility.

Vehicles

The park would need to purchase or lease tour vehicles large enough to accommodate the anticipated number of riders. The number of vehicles required will depend on intended frequency of service and the number of anticipated riders. Many of the stakeholders interviewed for *Report I* requested that smaller vehicles (maximum 30 passengers) be used for such a service, to minimize the traffic and parking impacts of the tour vehicles on the roads and in congested areas such as town centers. The vehicles may be outfitted with some on-board interpretive features such as audio systems and displays. The NPS can own these vehicles outright, or can lease vehicles from the U.S. General Services Administration (GSA) or a commercial service.

Vehicle Stops and Signposting

These are locations at key sites in and near Minute Man NHP where tour vehicles stop to load/unload passengers. These sites need to be large enough to accommodate the vehicles without significantly obstructing other vehicles visiting the sites. In some locations this might involve modifications to existing parking areas or the addition of new pullouts, although all the likely sites within Minute Man NHP (Minute Man Visitor Center, Hartwell Tavern, Meriam's Corner, North Bridge, and North Bridge Visitor Center) currently have adequate space in their parking areas and require minimal modifications. Adequate signage indicating the locations of tour vehicle stops and sheltered waiting areas with seating should also be provided at locations where visitors wait for vehicles.

Staffing

Drivers and interpretive guides are needed to staff the vehicles. As an alternative to guides, on-board automatic interpretive presentations can be used. Mechanics are needed to maintain the vehicles, and salespeople are also needed, to staff ticket sales locations. To minimize the demands placed on NPS staff, it is recommended that Minute Man NHP establish a concession agreement with a private company, whereby the outside company assumes responsibility for operating and maintaining the tour vehicles.

Storage and Maintenance Facility

This is a location where vehicles are stored when not in use. Facilities for performing routine vehicle maintenance should be co-located with the storage area, if possible. This site need not be within Minute Man NHP, but should be close enough to the tour route to minimize travel time and vehicle travel costs. Vehicle fueling also needs to be considered, including whether private fueling facilities should be built or if commercial filling stations are to be used.

Costs

Both the capital costs and operating costs of an interpretive tour service are substantial. It would be extremely difficult for Minute Man NHP to provide such a service on its own without partners. Many parks have been able to support successful tour services in partnership with other groups, including Valley Forge National Historical Park.

Capital costs include vehicles (if purchased outright), modifications to parking areas and signage at tour stop locations, any on-board interpretive systems intended for use, and a maintenance/storage facility (only applicable for purchased vehicles). Operating costs include staffing (drivers, interpretive staff, and ticket sales staff), fuel, and periodic maintenance/repair costs for the vehicles, and insurance. An analysis of Liberty Ride may provide insight on local costs of such a service.

There are several alternatives for the provision of vehicles, staffing, and vehicle maintenance, which have significantly different costs associated with them. The NPS and its partners can purchase vehicles, lease them, or contract with an outside company to provide vehicles. In the case of an outside company being hired, the company would likely be responsible for operations and maintenance as well. When selecting from among these options, Minute Man NHP should take into account the policies and regulations that govern the use of Alternative Transportation Program (ATP) funds. ATP money is limited to funding capital costs and may not be used for ongoing operating costs; the park and its partners need to cover operating costs with their regular annual operating budgets.

Revenues from tour ticket sales will help defray the cost of operating the tour service, but will not be able to cover all costs. Tour ticket prices can be estimated at $10-20, based on what the Liberty Ride and other tour services charge. The park and its partners need to anticipate contributing a significant amount to support the ongoing provision of the tour service.

Partners/Connectivity

Given the wealth of local historic sites around Minute Man NHP, there are excellent opportunities for partnerships. These include local towns, museums, historical preservation organizations, and chambers of commerce. Both Concord and Lexington expressed interest in a tour service that reduces private car traffic on their roads and brings visitors to their commercial areas around historic sites, and may be willing to contribute to support such a service.

Liberty Ride, Lexington's existing tour service, is a potential partner for service on a historic site-oriented route and may be willing to discuss a cooperative agreement with the NPS.

Hotels and other attractions may be willing to permit visitor parking in their lots, in exchange for being included in the shuttle route; this would provide another alternative for locating tour participant parking away from the park.

ATS Benefits

A service providing an interpretive bus tour offers a number of benefits to Minute Man NHP:

Traffic and Parking Congestion

A tour service could reduce private automobile traffic in and near Minute Man NHP, especially the number of cars turning onto and off of Route 2A, if the tour start/finish locations are at the far ends of the park. Locating the tour starting point even farther out (at the National Heritage Museum, for example) extends the benefits of congestion reduction even further. If the primary parking location is outside the park entirely, then the tour service could reduce the number of cars using parking lots at NPS sites. Tour users who begin their tour within the park create localized parking congestion as their vehicle stays in a single location throughout their trip as opposed to being moved as the visitor travels throughout the park.

Visitor Experience

A tour service provides a convenient means for visitors, especially those unfamiliar with the area, to travel between sites in and near the park. The on-board interpretation supplements interpretive services already provided by Minute Man NHP, and provides contact with a live interpreter during the ride who can provide additional information and answer questions. Tour participants will be permitted to exit vehicles at Minute Man NHP sites as they desire, so they will still have access to existing on-site services.

Park Resources

Reducing the number of cars traveling through the area around the park creates a safer and more pleasant environment. Fewer private cars reduce the need for turnouts and large parking lots throughout Minute Man NHP, enabling the park to dedicate more land to natural or interpretive settings. Noise and air pollution are also reduced.

It is not known whether a tour service would increase overall park visitation; improved services or better park access may attract new visitors. New visitation from a tour service, if any, would likely be less than 5% of total visitation and should not have a major impact on visitor centers and other on-site facilities. Tours do tend to group visitors into "pulses," which may pose a burden on some activities such as video presentations and tours of Hartwell Tavern.

Economic Development

The nearby commercial areas in Lexington and Concord both have limited public parking and are heavily congested, especially during the summer. A tour service offers a means for people to visit these areas and patronize shops and food services without placing a strain on the traffic and parking capacities of the towns.

Safety

The reduced private automobile traffic enabled by a tour service contributes to overall safety at the park. Fewer cars will be traveling on Route 2A and pulling into and out of parking areas along Route 2A and other local roads. Fewer cars in parking areas also reduce the opportunity for a pedestrian being struck by a driver looking for parking.

Riding in tour vehicles makes it possible for visitors to pay more attention safely to the surroundings and the sites, rather than trying to drive and sightsee at the same time.

A secondary safety benefit of tour vehicles is that they typically drive more slowly than private cars, and therefore will have a "traffic calming" effect on local roads.

Additional Evaluation Needed

Visitor demand for a tour service at Minute Man NHP needs to be evaluated and quantified. Market research needs to be conducted to determine whether a tour service is feasible, based on anticipated ticket revenues and overall cost. Visitor preferences for tour routes (desired stops) and overall duration need to be identified, to maximize customer satisfaction from the service. Visitors' willingness to pay for a tour also needs to be determined.

The Liberty Ride offers insight into the logistics of operating a tour service in the area. NPS should communicate with Liberty Ride staff, both to work towards establishing a partnership, as well as to learn from their experiences running a tour service.

Parking area usage throughout the park also needs to be studied, to determine where any parking shortages exist. This will help to determine both the proper locations for tour vehicle stops and likely spots for tour participant parking.

ATP Qualification

Capital costs qualify for ATP funds, but ongoing operations costs have to be covered by other funding sources within the NPS and its partners. Eligible items for ATP funding include vehicles, road and parking area modifications, waiting area signage and facilities, and any vehicle-support buildings or facilities.

Sample Tour Itineraries

The following are two possible itineraries for a tour service in the Minute Man NHP area. The first is a route serving only Minute Man NHP and Concord Town Center. The second route covers both Concord and Lexington, and is based on the existing Liberty Ride service. Both routes are illustrated in Map 2.

1. *Minute Man NHP and Concord Town Center*

At a minimum, a tour service should cover the most popular sites within Minute Man NHP. It also makes sense for the tour route to include Concord Town Center, since the travel route between the two main units of the park passes through the town. Based on park visitor data, one viable itinerary that incorporates the most popular sites is the following (assuming an east-to-west route):

1. Minute Man Visitor Center
2. Hartwell Tavern
3. The Wayside/Orchard House
4. Concord Town Center
5. North Bridge/Old Manse
6. North Bridge Visitor Center

These represent the bare minimum of stop locations, based on visitor popularity and reasonable walking distance to other sites along the Battle Road Trail. Other sites could be added as tour duration permits; Fiske Hill, the Paul Revere capture site, and Meriam's Corner are potential additions to the route.

This itinerary has a duration of approximately 60 minutes round-trip, depending on local traffic conditions and the amount of time the vehicle waits at each stop. This enables the tour service to have departures every hour, or every 30 minutes if two vehicles are used. The number of daily departures can be adjusted to meet visitor demand, but the NPS should anticipate providing service between 10:00 am and 4:00 pm throughout the peak season.

Based on comparisons with existing bus and walking interpretive tours, the NPS can charge an admission price of $10-20 per adult. This fee provides people with access to the tour vehicle(s) throughout the day (unlimited boardings and alightings) and the interpretive information presented en route.

Managing parking for the tours within the park may be a challenge. Tour participants can park their cars at Minute Man Visitor Center or the North Bridge Visitor Center parking area, although these lots have difficulty accommodating self-driven visitors during peak seasons. Ideally, Minute Man NHP would be able to partner with nearby organizations and share their facilities when not in use. Churches, schools, office complexes or other historical facilities may have parking available.

The benefits of this route are that it covers the areas required for visitors to see the park and confers some congestion reduction, resource preservation and visitor experience benefits, while minimizing operating costs. The route offers a partnership opportunity with the town of Concord, while not requiring use of the limited public parking in Concord Town Center. Focusing on park sites saves over four miles of travel as compared to a service that connected to Lexington Town Center as well; this allows fewer vehicles to provide more tours. The primary disadvantage is that it does not include sites in Lexington, potentially alienating visitors interested in seeing sites in both towns and eliminating the opportunity for a partnership with the town of Lexington. Many visitors come to see "Lexington-and-Concord," which they consider to be a single destination.

Map 2
Tour Route Options for Minute Man NHP
Base Map Source: National Park Service

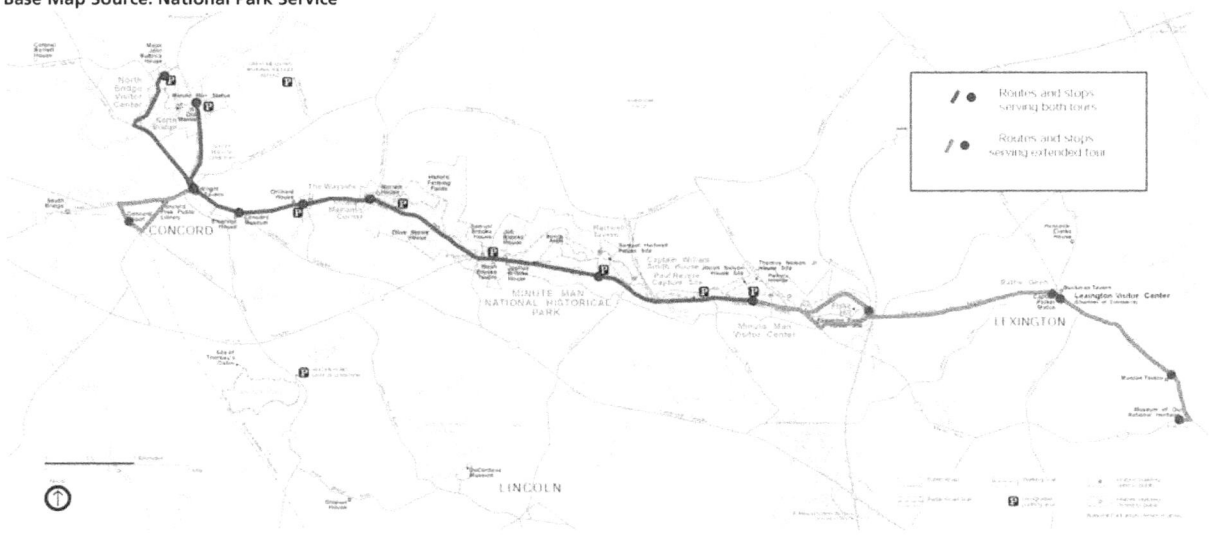

2. Lexington and Concord: the Liberty Ride Model

A second, longer option is a route that includes historic sites in Lexington and additional stops within the park to the above itinerary. The Liberty Ride commercial tour service currently offers a similar route, and the NPS should investigate the possibility of partnering with the Liberty Ride and its supporters to ensure the route includes the desired sites within the park.

Vehicles could cover a ninety-minute to two-hour route that starts and finishes at the National Heritage Museum, and includes the following stops:

1. National Heritage Museum
2. Lexington Visitor Center/Lexington Battle Green area
3. Fiske Hill
4. Minute Man Visitor Center
5. Hartwell Tavern
6. Meriam's Corner
7. Orchard House/Wayside
8. Concord Town Center
9. North Bridge/Old Manse
10. North Bridge Visitor Center
11. Concord Depot
12. Concord Museum/Emerson's House
13. Lexington Belfry
14. Munroe Tavern

This itinerary offers a "one-stop shopping" solution to visitors who desire a comprehensive visit to all the significant historic sites in the Lexington/Concord area. The tour starts and finishes at the National Heritage Museum to take advantage of its plentiful parking and to minimize the burden placed on parking areas in the Lexington and Concord town centers and Minute Man NHP.

Depending on the precise length of the tour and number of vehicles, tours could be scheduled hourly using two vehicles or every ninety minutes or two hours using a single bus. Currently

Liberty Ride charges $20 for adults and $10 for children 5-17 years old and tickets are valid for two consecutive days and include free re-boarding, enabling them to get on and off and spend as much time at any site as they desire.

The benefits of a longer route are that it provides a more comprehensive interpretive experience to visitors, offering a detailed account of the events in Lexington and Concord that led to the American Revolution. It encourages people to park their cars a significant distance from Minute Man NHP, thereby improving parking and traffic conditions near the park, yet offers visitors enough flexibility to adjust the duration of their participation in the tour as they desire. The longer route also offers partnership opportunities with the towns of both Lexington and Concord and the existing Liberty Ride tour incorporates sites from both communities. The disadvantages of the longer route are increased operating tour cycle time, leading to increased operating costs and the need for additional vehicles in order to maintain headways of 60 minutes.

II. Shuttle Bus Service Options

General Description

A shuttle bus service provides transportation to and through the park at regular intervals, with stops at strategic locations. In comparison to a tour service, a shuttle's primary purpose is transportation and it offers little or no interpretation, instead focusing on providing an efficient means for people to travel within the area. This service offers greater flexibility in timing, routes and destinations than an interpretive bus tour, and appeals to a broader audience. Shuttle passengers can be given the option of purchasing "point-to-point" tickets for one-time use, all-day passes valid on all vehicles, or even seasonal passes for commuter use.

As with a tour service, it is highly unlikely that the Minute Man NHP would be able to bear the cost of operating and sustaining such a system on its own and would need to partner with other local interested entities.

Geography

A shuttle service can serve four types of destinations in the Minute Man NHP area:

I. Historic sites

Routes focusing on historic sites include stops at local sites of historical or cultural interest, which are the primary attractions in the area. Minute Man NHP, the town of Concord, and the town of Lexington all have destinations in this category. These sites appeal primarily to tourists and other visitors interested in learning about the area's history.

II. Nearby transit connections

MBTA provides commuter rail and bus service adjacent to the park. The purpose of including these destinations in a shuttle route is to establish a link between the nearby transit services, Minute Man NHP, and other local destinations.

Shuttle connections to local transit make it much more convenient for someone to visit the park without any use of a private car. This makes the park accessible to tourists and others in the Boston area without cars. It also appeals to local residents near the park who could use the shuttle as part of their work commute into the Boston area. Currently there is no public transportation service connecting Lexington and Concord Town Centers.

III. Commercial areas

Shuttle routes can include the town centers of Concord and Lexington, to provide riders with access to local shops and food services. These sites appeal to tourists (who may want to buy food or other supplies midway through their tour of the area), and may also attract some local residents who live on or near the shuttle route and can use it as a convenient method to reach the town centers.

In Lexington's case, the town center is co-located with the Battle Green and visitor center and a single stop serves all destinations. A shuttle stop in Concord Town Center does not require any additional travel for a route including both the Battle Road and North Bridge units of Minute Man NHP, since the most direct route between the two units passes through the town center.

IV. Local Employment Centers

There are several local employment centers in the area whose employees might use a shuttle that connects their workplaces with local transit. Hanscom AFB operates a very limited shuttle service, and may be interested in a partnership with the NPS. Additional development of the air force base would provide additional demand. There are also several office parks on Virginia Road that could be served by a commuter-specific route during peak hours in the mornings and evenings.

Routes can serve any combination of these destinations, and can vary over the course of the day and season. Including (or excluding) each type of destination affects some of the characteristics of the shuttle service; some of these differences are highlighted in the sample shuttle itineraries at the end of this section.

As with a tour service, expanding the route of the shuttle farther from a "core" Minute Man NHP route increases the cycle time of the vehicle, decreases the frequency of shuttle service, but serves a broader pool of potential riders. The inclusion of non-NPS sites also increases partnership opportunities with local towns and other agencies.

Shuttles are intended to serve continuous routes without specific "start/finish" locations. This characteristic helps reduce parking congestion in any one place by distributing visitor parking among multiple sites. However, the NPS still needs to include parking locations with the capacity to accommodate a large number of cars, since the cars will remain in place for some time while their owners use the shuttle; churches, schools, office complexes or other historical facilities may be willing to share parking.

Audience

A shuttle provides service that appeals to a broad customer base, depending on the timing of routes and the stops included in the route. Shuttle service appeals to riders who want more flexibility in their travel schedule while in the park. These include history enthusiasts who desire a convenient means to travel among the NPS sites and are less concerned with receiving interpretive information, as well as commuters and incidental local users traveling to/from local employment centers and transportation hubs.

Timing

Shuttle service should follow a regular schedule (e.g., every 15 minutes) during peak season and a reduced schedule during "shoulder" seasons, as dictated by demand. In comparison to a tour bus service, a shuttle should have a shorter headway (maximum of 15-20 minutes) and stop at more locations in order to serve its intended ridership more effectively. The shorter the headway, the more likely people are to use the service.

Consideration should also be given to varying the frequency and routes of vehicles over the course of the day, depending on the target audience(s). If, for example, the shuttle is intended to serve local residents using the commuter rail to travel to work in Boston, shuttles should make more frequent pick-up/drop-offs at the Concord Depot on weekday mornings and evenings than may be justified at other times of the day and week. Since the majority of park visitors do not arrive until after the visitor centers open (9am during peak season), it is feasible to operate the shuttles with different routes during the mornings and evenings than during the day.

Interpretation

A shuttle service emphasizes transportation as its primary benefit, and therefore offers limited interpretive services, if any. Minimal travel time between stops, as well as cost, make live and/or audio interpretation unattractive, but some information can be provided through printed materials or personal audio devices carried on-board. Shuttle riders receive interpretive information at many of the sites within the park, so there is not a critical need to provide such service on-board the shuttle.

Infrastructure

Shuttle bus service requires the same four principal types of infrastructure as bus tour service. There are, however, a few differences:

Vehicles

Due to shorter headways, a shuttle service requires more vehicles than the tour service options described in the previous section. Shuttle vehicles should be designed for easier boardings and alightings, and should include standing room to accommodate higher numbers of passengers. Comfort and visibility out of the vehicle are less of a concern for shuttle vehicles because passengers spend less time inside. Bike racks on the vehicles would allow visitors to bike through the park in one direction without retracing their route.

Vehicle Stops and Signposting

The stop location requirements for shuttle vehicles are very similar to those for tour vehicles. To support shorter stops at each site, shuttle pick-up/drop off points should be streamlined to enable easier entry and exit with less interference from other vehicles.

Staffing

As with tour vehicles, vehicle drivers and maintenance staff are needed, although interpretive staff are not required. The need for staff can be addressed through a concession agreement with a private company, if desired.

Storage and Maintenance Facility

Since more vehicles are needed to support a shuttle service with short headways, the storage facility must be large enough to accommodate the appropriate number of vehicles.

Costs

Both the capital costs and operating costs of a shuttle service are substantial. It is unlikely that the NPS can provide such a service on its own without partners, or even to be the primary contributor to the expense of such a system. Aside from the lack of need for interpretive staff, both the capital and operating costs for a shuttle service will be higher than for a tour service, since a greater number of vehicles are used, and operating hours will probably be longer.

Capital costs include vehicles (if purchased outright), modifications to parking areas and signage at tour stop locations, any on-board interpretive materials intended for use, and a maintenance/storage facility (only applicable for purchased vehicles). Operating costs include staffing (drivers, mechanics, and ticket sales staff), fuel, periodic maintenance/repair costs for the vehicles, and insurance.

There are several alternatives for the provision of vehicles, staffing, and vehicle maintenance, which have significantly different costs associated with them. The NPS and its partners can purchase vehicles, lease them, or contract with an outside company to provide vehicles. In the case of an outside company being hired, the company would likely be responsible for operations and maintenance as well. When selecting from among these options, Minute Man NHP should take into account the policies and regulations that govern the use of ATP funds. ATP money is limited to funding capital costs and may not be used for ongoing operating costs; the park and its partners need to cover operating costs with their regular annual operating budgets.

Revenues from shuttle ticket sales can help defray the cost of operating the tour service, but assuming a ticket price is even charged, its contribution to covering overhead will be minimal. Market research is needed to determine what fee is acceptable to visitors; it is possible visitors may find any fee unacceptable and will choose to drive instead. In any event, the park and its partners need to anticipate contributing a significant amount to support the ongoing provision of the shuttle service.

ATS Benefits

A shuttle service providing transportation throughout the area offers a number of benefits to Minute Man NHP:

Traffic and Parking Congestion

A shuttle service's benefits may be more noticeable when used to transport commuters during rush hour congestion. It reduces private automobile traffic in and near Minute Man NHP, especially the number of cars turning onto and off of Route 2A. Locating the primary parking site(s) farther from the park extends the benefits of traffic congestion reduction even further.

A shuttle service reduces the number of cars using parking lots at NPS sites, particularly at those sites located midway along the Battle Road unit of the park. This benefit is magnified if the primary parking location(s) are located outside the park entirely.

Connections to alternative transportation such as the Concord Depot completely eliminates the need for visitors to drive.

Visitor Experience

A shuttle service provides a convenient means for visitors, especially those unfamiliar with the area, to travel between sites in and near the park. Reducing traffic and parking congestion makes the overall experience more pleasant for all visitors, whether they are riding the shuttle or driving their own cars. The shuttle service enables people to exit the vehicle and spend time at any of the stops, so visitors are still able to take advantage of existing on-site services and interpretation.

Park Resources

Reducing the number of cars traveling through the area around the park creates a safer and more pleasant environment. Having fewer private cars reduces the need for larger parking lots throughout Minute Man NHP, enabling the park to dedicate more land to natural or interpretive settings. Noise and air pollution are also reduced. A shuttle service may be able to attract locals, reducing the number of non-trips made along Route 2A further.

A shuttle will provide better access to visitors without cars, but it is not known how much a shuttle service would increase overall park visitation; improved services or better park access may attract new visitors. New visitation from a shuttle service, if any, would likely be less than 5% of total visitation and should not have a major impact on visitor centers and other on-site facilities. Shuttle do tend to group visitors into "pulses," which may pose a burden on some activities such as video presentations and tours of Hartwell Tavern.

Economic Development

The nearby commercial areas in Lexington and Concord both have limited public parking and are heavily congested, especially during the summer. A shuttle service offers a means for people to visit these areas and patronize shops and food services without placing a strain on the traffic and parking capacities of the towns. Such a service may attract local travelers, increasing access to commerce between the two towns. Transit access is also of some benefit to local employers, who can offer it as a fringe benefit to their staff.

Safety

The reduced private automobile traffic enabled by a shuttle service contributes to overall safety at the park. Fewer private cars will be traveling on Route 2A and pulling into and out of parking areas along Route 2A and other local roads. Fewer cars in parking areas also reduce the likelihood of a pedestrian being struck by a driver looking for parking.

Riding in tour vehicles makes it possible for visitors to pay more attention safely to the surroundings and the sites, rather than trying to drive and sightsee at the same time.

A secondary safety benefit of shuttle vehicles is that they typically drive more slowly than private cars, and therefore will have a "traffic calming" effect on local roads.

Additional Evaluation Needed

Visitor demand for a shuttle service at Minute Man NHP needs to be evaluated and quantified. Market research needs to be conducted to determine whether a tour service is feasible, based on anticipated ticket revenues and overall cost. Visitor preferences for shuttle routes (desired stops) and overall cycle duration need to be identified, to maximize customer satisfaction from the service. Visitors' willingness to pay for a tour also needs to be determined.

Explore partnership opportunities with local towns, agencies and businesses. Consider these from the aspects of financial participation in the shuttle service and targeted marketing opportunities for ridership (hotel guests, commuters, etc.).

ATP Qualification

Capital costs qualify for ATP funds, but ongoing operational costs have to be covered by other funding sources within the NPS and its partners. Eligible items for ATP funding include vehicles, road and parking area modifications, waiting area signage and facilities, and any vehicle-support buildings or facilities.

Sample Shuttle Routes

The following are possible routes for a shuttle service in the Minute Man NHP area. Each illustrates the logistics of serving different sets of audiences, and the benefits and drawbacks of different routes. Map 3 shows the different routing options.

1. Minute Man NHP and Concord Town Center

A shuttle service should, at a minimum, travel to all of the sites within Minute Man NHP. It makes sense to include Concord Town Center, since the route between the two main units of the park passes directly through the town. Based on an east-to-west route, the itinerary can include the following:

1. Fiske Hill
2. Minute Man Visitor Center
3. Paul Revere Capture Site
4. Hartwell Tavern
5. Samuel Brooks House

6. Meriam's Corner
7. The Wayside
8. Concord Town Center
9. North Bridge/Old Manse
10. North Bridge Visitor Center

This route has a cycle duration of approximately 45 minutes, depending on local traffic conditions and the amount of time the vehicle waits at each stop. The number of daily departures can be adjusted to meet visitor demand, but the NPS should anticipate providing service with a maximum headway of 15-20 minutes between 10am and 4pm throughout the peak season, requiring a minimum of three vehicles.

The NPS has to decide whether it will charge a ticket fee for riding this shuttle. While some portion of visitors are likely willing to pay for an all-day pass to ride unlimited shuttles, visitors who enjoy this service free of charge at other parks, such as Acadia and Yosemite, may be upset about having to pay for the shuttle at Minute Man NHP and choose to use their own car instead.

Tour participants can park their cars at any parking area along the route. It is preferable, however, to arrange for parking outside of the route. It is unlikely that parking areas within the park have sufficient capacity to accommodate the cars of shuttle riders and self-driven visitors during peak season.

The benefits of this route are that it provides a means for visitors to travel throughout the entire park and confers some congestion reduction, resource preservation and visitor experience benefits, while minimizing operating costs. The route offers a partnership opportunity with the town of Concord, while not placing a burden on the limited public parking in Concord Town Center. The primary disadvantage of the route is that it does not include sites in Lexington, which many visitors see as a key part of their visit, and eliminates the opportunity for a partnership with the town of Lexington. It also does not take advantage of the opportunities to serve local residents and park visitors who want to use transit to travel to or from the area.

2. Commuter Service

A supplemental route can connect local employment centers to the commuter rail station. Hanscom AFB currently provides pick-up service and expressed interest in coordinating with a NPS shuttle service. Additional employers along Virginia Road or near the intersection of Marrett Road and Massachusetts Avenue may also be interested in developing an employee shuttle.

The purpose of adding these stops is to make the shuttle more supportive of local residents traveling to work in the Boston area via transit, and connect local employers to existing transit services. While a commuter service does not directly impact park visitors, it provides an opportunity to partner with the local community businesses and may allow the service to be financially feasible.

Incorporating a commuter shuttle service allows the same vehicle to be used for two different routes used at different times during the day.

Daytime Hours (10am – 4pm):

During the day, the shuttle operates on a very similar schedule to the first sample itinerary. An additional stop could be added at Concord Depot, ideally timed to match the arrivals and departures of commuter rail trains; this should add about 5-10 minutes to the cycle duration. Unfortunately, this extra time may require an additional vehicle to be purchased to keep frequent headways. During these hours, the focus of the service is still on moving visitors to different park sites.

Peak Commute Hours (6:30am – 10am and 4pm – 7pm):

During the peak commute hours, the routing and headway of the shuttle changes significantly. Since there are few, if any, visitors to the park during these times, the focus of the service is on moving commuters to and from transit connections. Stops at Concord Depot and local employment centers (Hanscom AFB and business parks on Virginia Road) become the priority.

Map 3
Shuttle Route Options for Minute Man NHP, Concord Town Center and Transit Connections
Base Map Source: National Park Service

This shuttle system can have a variable fee structure. Regular daytime riders are charged the same fee as under the previous example, and commuters have the option to buy a monthly pass for the shuttle service. Monthly passes are preferable because they provide a steadier income stream and encourage people to use the service more regularly once they have committed themselves by buying a pass.

This combination of routes confers all of the benefits of the first shuttle itinerary, and attracts a larger potential ridership by targeting transit users and local employees. It also opens up the opportunity for a partnership with Hanscom AFB and other employment centers. The disadvantages of this system are that operating costs are increased and operations become more complex: vehicles schedules need to be coordinated with the arrivals and departures of commuter rail trains, which may require more vehicles. Staffing the service also becomes more complicated because additional drivers may be needed to keep the vehicle in service for more than eight hours each day.

3. Lexington and Concord, with or without transit connections

A third, longer option is a route that again focuses on historic sites, but includes additional stops at historic locations in Lexington. This greatly expands the service area of the shuttle, drawing on a broader potential ridership and meeting many visitors' expectations of seeing both Concord and Lexington. In addition, this route fills a missing transit connection between the two town centers and may appeal to some local residents interested in traveling between the two.

The route can extend as far east as the National Heritage Museum and include the following stops:

1. National Heritage Museum
2. Munroe Tavern

3. Lexington Visitor Center/Lexington Battle Green area
4. Fiske Hill
5. Minute Man Visitor Center
6. Paul Revere Capture Site
7. Hartwell Tavern
8. Samuel Brooks
9. Meriam's Corner
10. The Wayside
11. Concord Museum/Emerson's House
12. Concord Town Center
13. Concord Depot
14. North Bridge/Old Manse
15. North Bridge Visitor Center

This route offers tourists a comprehensive visit to all the significant historic sites in the Lexington/Concord area. The inclusion of the National Heritage Museum in the route takes advantage of its plentiful parking and could minimize the burden placed on parking areas in the Lexington and Concord town centers and in Minute Man NHP.

The main challenge of such a route is maintaining short enough headways for a shuttle service: a maximum of 15-20 minutes between shuttles is still the goal. Given the length of the route, a minimum of six vehicles is required. One way to alleviate this problem is to shorten the cycle duration by eliminating some of the less popular stops within the park, especially those that are within convenient walking distance of more important sites where the shuttle stops.

This route can also be combined with the transit-focused schedule described in the previous example. During morning and evening peak commute times, vehicles can be used to transport people between transit connections and local homes/businesses. Stops at historic sites can be minimized or eliminated. As with the Concord-only transit-centric route, the headways must remain short enough to make the service viable for commuters on tight time schedules, especially in the morning.

The benefits of a longer route are that it provides a more comprehensive experience to visitors, offering a full view of the significant sites in Lexington and Concord. It encourages people to park their cars a significant distance from Minute Man NHP or to forego a car entirely, thereby improving parking and traffic conditions near the park, yet offers visitors enough flexibility to adjust the duration of their visit as desired. The longer route also offers partnership opportunities with the towns of both Lexington and Concord and provides the sole public transportation option between the two town centers. The disadvantages of the route are increased route cycle time, leading to increased operating costs and the need for an additional vehicle to provide timely service.

III. Pedestrian Options

General Description

When considering walking as an alternative transportation service at Minute Man NHP, there are two issues to consider: First, can people access the park without a car? Second, is it possible to travel throughout the park without a vehicle?

The park's linear nature and multiple units make walking-only trips difficult. Improvements to the pedestrian environment are geared toward making the park available to those who choose to walk and encouraging walking as a supplement to other alternative transportation services.

Geography

Being central to the park's three units, Concord Town Center serves as the focal point of pedestrian access to the park.

North Bridge Unit

The North Bridge Unit, the most popular in the park, is located approximately 1 ¼ miles from the Concord train depot and just over a half mile from downtown Concord. Sidewalks exist on at least one side of the streets in this area. Pedestrians are left to fend for themselves just south of the Reformatory Branch Trail, where the sidewalk switches from one side of Monument Street to the other, since there are no crosswalks signage or signalization at this location. A crosswalk is marked between the North Bridge parking lot and the bridge itself. Footpaths cross the North Bridge Unit providing direct access between the visitor center and bridge.

Wayside and Battle Road Units

Sidewalks extend along one side of Lexington Road between Concord Town Center and Meriam's Corner, the western tip of the Battle Road Unit. Midway, at the Wayside, crosswalks are marked from the Wayside Parking lot across Lexington Road to the historical houses. Crosswalks are provided at the intersection of Old Bedford Road and Lexington Road to allow pedestrian access at Meriam's Corner. Traffic speeds along Lexington Road and the distance between Concord Center and the Battle Road Unit deter pedestrian access to the Battle Road Unit. Once within the Battle Road Unit, the Battle Road Trail provides an excellent pedestrian experience for those willing and able to walk sections or its entire 5.5-mile length.

Transit Connections

Concord Depot is the nearest stop for the MBTA Commuter Rail, and is approximately 0.5 miles from Concord Town Center. As it is contained within Concord's "urban" grid, the Depot is connected to the town center by sidewalks and crosswalks.

An alternative for car-less visitors to the park is to take the No. 76 bus to Marrett Road and Old Massachusetts Avenue A crosswalk is provided to assist visitors crossing from the bus stop to the walking trail that connects to the Battle Road Trail.

Audience

The linear nature of the park and distances between units make it challenging to visit the park without a car. Rangers report occasionally meeting visitors at the North Bridge who have walked to the park from the Concord Depot commuter rail station, usually fewer than two groups per month. While walking alone may not be a feasible means to visit the park, improvements to the walking environment encourage walking as a supplement to other alternative transportation services. Visitors can walk between some sites without being constrained by shuttle or tour routes and schedules.

Employees from nearby office parks and residents living adjacent to the park often walk to the Battle Road Unit. The Battle Road Trail is popular with both visitors exploring the history of the park and local residents who visit the park to walk or bike recreationally. No information is known as to the number of people who walk the entire stretch of the Battle Road Trail, or which segments are the most popular, but it is estimated that upwards of 300,000 people annually use some portion of the Battle Road Trail.

Timing

While walking provides one of the more sensory and deliberate park experiences, it is a slow method of travel, with people averaging only three miles per hour. Table 3 provides estimated walking times for different trip segments, not including time for stops to visit and learn about the many sites along the way.

Table 3
Walking Distance and Times Between Sites

Segment	Distance	Estimated Time
Concord Depot to Concord Center	0.5 miles	10 minutes
Concord Center to the North Bridge	0.75 miles	15 minutes
Concord Center to The Wayside	0.9 miles	18 minutes
Wayside to Meriam's Corner	0.45 miles	9 minutes
Meriam's Corner to Hartwell Tavern (via Battle Road Trail)	2.75 miles	55 minutes
Hartwell Tavern to Minute Man Visitor Center (via Battle Road Trail)	1.8 miles	36 minutes
Minute Man Visitor Center to Fiske Hill (via Battle Road Trail)	0.9 miles	18 minutes

The 15-mile round trip from Concord Depot to Fiske Hill takes almost five hours just to walk. For a fit group, this is a feasible all-day activity but is unlikely to attract a high percentage of visitors.

One benefit of walking is that it can be done individually without constraint of a schedule. For this reason, walking between some sites in combination with a shuttle service provides additional freedom for visitors and minimizes the amount of time needed to wait for transportation.

Interpretation

Walking allows visitors to immerse themselves in the 18th and 19th century experiences the park provides as well as to enjoy the natural beauty of the area. The visitor centers, house tours and interpretive signage support pedestrian visitation at the park. The deliberate nature of walking makes smaller passive displays highly effective. The park currently has three audio tours available to visitors through their personal cell phones. Other venues such as museums rely on park-owned hand held devices, which do not require visitors to own a cell phone but require collecting them at the end of the visitor's trip.

Scheduled walking tours of limited areas of the park encourage walking from site to site and enhance the interpretive experience. Ranger-led interpretive trail walks are extremely popular and are offered without charge. The schedule of these tours is currently limited due to staffing constraints. The Concord Chamber of Commerce also provides three different walking tour options, each approximately 1.5 hours long. The tours run twice a day on weekends and holidays and once a day on weekdays from April 15th through October 31. The Chamber charges $15 for adults, $10 for students and seniors, and $5 for children under 12.

Map 4
Key Walking Routes (indicated in red) between Concord Depot, Concord Town Center and Minute Man NHP
(Battle Road Trail indicated with blue dashed line)
Base Map Source: National Park Service

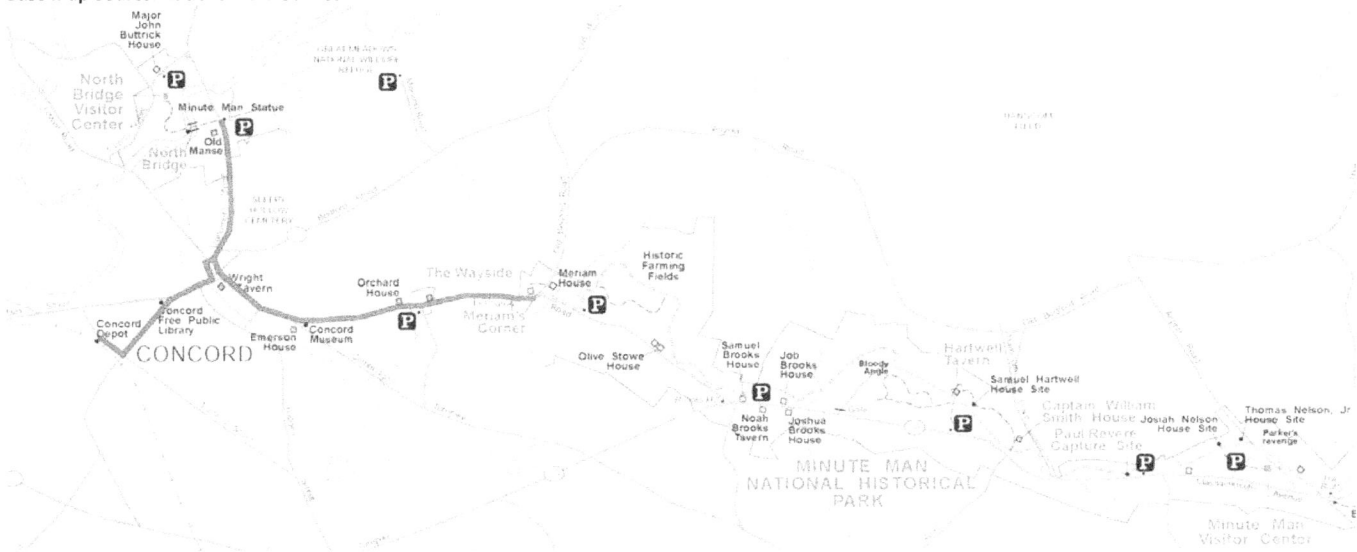

Infrastructure

The infrastructure required for walking is relatively minimal but includes:

Sidewalks and paths

Ensuring a safe, relatively smooth pathway is of primary concern. The Battle Road Trail and pathways within the North Bridge Unit of the park provide a good network for walking within the park. Map 4 indicates pathways that are of primary concern when trying to provide connections between the park units and Concord Town Center. Sidewalks exist on one side of the streets connecting Concord Center to the North Bridge Unit and The Wayside. Massachusetts Avenue (Route 2A), classified as an urban minor arterial, does not have sidewalks on the section west of Route 128, which makes pedestrian access between local businesses and the park difficult. Legally, pedestrian (and bicycle) accommodation should be made along this road where feasible. Scenic Byway designation may provide grounds for not adding pedestrian accommodations. Two areas where pedestrian improvements should be made include 1) adding a crosswalk on Monument St. near the North Bridge where the sidewalk switches from one side of the road to the other and 2) extending the sidewalks on Marrett Road to connect with the walking path at Old Massachusetts Avenue Currently the sidewalks end at the Sheraton Lexington Inn driveway and Cranberry Hill Road and the only crosswalk spanning Marrett Road is at the Sheraton Lexington Inn.

When adding sidewalks and other pedestrian infrastructure, it is important to consider that it needs to be compatible with the 18th and 19th century landscape the park is trying to preserve. The park and others will need to discuss the safety and transportation benefits of new infrastructure with the historical context.

Signage/interpretation

Signage directing pedestrians from one area of the park to another with distances listed helps visitors find their way and schedule their visit, letting them know the ease or difficulty of reaching the next site.

Current pedestrian signage within the Battle Road Unit is excellent. Signs at the Minute Man Visitor Center Parking Lot provide distance and time estimates for the walk from the parking lot to the visitor center. Granite posts along the original Battle Road route note distances to major sites such as Boston Harbor and Meriam's Corner, a concept which could be expanded to provide additional distance information.

During the initial phase of this project, the Concord Chamber of Commerce acknowledged that there is insufficient visitor-oriented signage within the town center. Improving pedestrian information for travel between the Concord Depot, Concord Town Center and the North Bridge and Wayside Units physically connects the town center to the park and encourages walking visits by people who might otherwise drive. Additional signage also acts as advertising, possibly even prompting impromptu visits to the park.

Signage is also needed to encourage use of the footpath between the North Bridge and North Bridge Visitor Center.

Marker on the Battle Road Trail

Visitor amenities

Existing visitor facilities located throughout the park, including bathrooms, picnic benches, and water fountains, make extended visits to the park more comfortable. A survey of visitors could help determine if and where additional facilities are needed. Food and beverage services are often requested by Battle Road Trail users in particular. Several historic structures located along the trail could be used to provide these services.

Costs

Capital Costs

Completing the sidewalk network and enhancing visitor safety at street crossings using crosswalks, yield signs or other techniques could require considerable expense, especially if the width of the right of way is limited. Currently, Route 2A does not include pedestrian amenities. Since it was recently repaved, it is unlikely that the Commonwealth would consider adding sidewalks in the near future. Striping crosswalks at key locations noted earlier would provide major safety benefits, be significantly less expensive, and could be done quickly. A Town of Concord Planning Department representative acknowledged that there were insufficient connections between recreational facilities when contacted during Volpe's inventory of existing conditions. Minute Man NHP needs to work with Concord and other towns as well as with the Massachusetts Highway Department to improve this infrastructure, as it falls outside of the park's jurisdiction.

The cost of interpretive amenities such as signs, displays, and audio interpretation varies, depending on their size, numbers, and level of sophistication.

Operating Costs

Aside from guided walking tours, amenities for walkers do not require significant operating costs. Maintenance of sidewalks and paths make up the largest on-going costs.

Pricing

Since most pedestrian trips are difficult to monitor, opportunities for collecting revenue from walking trips are slim. If desired, a fee could be levied on guided walking tours or audio interpretation. Concord Chamber of Commerce currently charges $15 for their local tours. The park's existing cell phone tours cost $5.99 for two tours, plus any applicable cell phone airtime and roaming. Museums charge up to $5 for their hand-held devices.

Partners/Connectivity

The Town of Concord is the local stakeholder most likely to be interested in improving pedestrian access to the park, since its boundaries encompass the likely walking routes and it owns most of the relevant right-of-ways. Lexington and Lincoln should be involved with providing better access to the Battle Road Trail. The Massachusetts Highway Department needs to be involved if any changes are proposed for Route 2A.

ATS Benefits

While it is unlikely that walking will become a predominant means of travel to the park, it is an important mode to consider. In combination with other alternative transportation systems, walking provides the opportunity to experience all the park has to offer. Signage, maps and cultural acceptance of walking between sites can increase pedestrian use of the park where visitors currently drive. It is important to remember that the National Park Service Alternative Transportation Program will fund improvements that provide transportation benefits, but not those that primarily benefit the hiking and touring experience.

Traffic and Parking Congestion

Increased pedestrian activity is unlikely to have much impact on traffic or parking congestion although it reduces the number of short driving trips made within the park, minimizing the potential for incidents as vehicles pull on and off route 2A.

Visitor Experience

Walking between sites reduces the number of times a visitor must get in and out of a vehicle for short trips, allowing them to more fully absorb the historic environment. Walking allows access to parts of the park inaccessible by other means. The linear nature of the park makes returning to one's vehicle after seeing the park by foot, a significant disincentive to walk unless additional alternative transportation services are provided to fill this need.

Park Resources

Since it is expected walk-only visits to the park are limited, walking will not reduce impacts to the park from vehicles. Few negative impacts on the park are seen from improving the existing pedestrian infrastructure since it is generally adequate within the park. Street crossings and sidewalks along Route 2A may conflict with the historic nature of the park unless very carefully implemented. Scenic Byway designation for 2A may provide the park with protection against visually undesirable improvements, but may also make it more difficult to add safety features. Additional pathways within the park could expand access with only minor changes to the existing landscape.

Economic Development

Improved pedestrian connections to Concord may provide a small increase in walking trips between Minute Man NHP and the town center; this in turn encourages use of the MBTA Commuter Rail to access the park and provides visitors additional opportunities to shop at the local businesses.

Safety

Safety benefits of encouraging walking include reducing the number of vehicles pulling on and off Route 2A. Constructing sidewalks and improving roadway crossings where needed prevents pedestrian-auto incidents. Residents and workers increasingly cross Route 2A on foot or bike without the benefit of crosswalks.

Additional Evaluation Needed

Data on the number of people using the Battle Road Trail and the length and purpose of their trips is needed to provide information as to how visitors are currently using the facilities and how to direct additional resources to better meet pedestrian needs.

ATP Qualification

Pedestrian improvements connecting the park to the Concord Depot (or downtown Concord), such as sidewalks and directional signage, may be considered for ATP funds, especially if jointly financed by the Town of Concord. Other pedestrian improvements, especially those related to improved interpretation, are less likely to receive ATP funds as they relate more to interpretation than transportation.

IV. Bicycle Options

General Description

Biking, as opposed to walking, may be the best non-motorized transportation option for Minute Man NHP because it significantly reduces travel times between sites. Nearby paths, trails and other bikeable routes make bicycling to the park a viable alternative to driving to the park.[13] Recreational cycling is a popular activity both on the bike paths and on local public roads.

This section focuses on non-scheduled and independent bike use to and within the park. Organized bike tours have been attempted in the past, with the park offering an on-site tour and a commercial operator visiting the park as a part of a longer tour of Lexington and Concord. More information needs to be collected on past uses of organized bike tours to determine if they were well received and economically feasible. Improvements discussed in this section are beneficial to any organized tour, although more focus needs to be placed on the experience of on-road riding between park units and other bike paths for groups.

Geography

Bikeable routes are available both within the park and for accessing the park. In addition to the Battle Road Trail, connections between Lexington Center, Bedford Depot/Reformatory Branch, Concord Depot and each of the park units should be considered as potential bicycle routes in the context of ATP.

In-Park

Within the park, the Battle Road Trail supports bike touring of the park, providing similar access to walking, but with faster travel. The Battle Road Trail's unpaved surface allows for biking at slower speeds. Maintenance of some of the sandier sections of the trail is needed to accommodate bikes with skinnier tires. Route 2A is a poor alternative to the Battle Road Trail for most cyclists, as there are no bike lanes and vehicle traffic moves quickly. When traveling west to east, turning in and out of the parking areas across traffic lanes on Route 2A to access the parking areas, which are on the north side of the road, is dangerous for cyclists.

Biking is of less benefit at the North Bridge and Wayside Units, which are much smaller and are just as convenient for walkers as for cyclists. Local bike organizations do, however, identify the path through the North Bridge Unit as a part of the bike network. Improvements to either this path or the roads around the North Bridge Unit benefit cyclists.

---

[13] It is assumed that bikers have some comfort level with street biking. Most roadways between units have sidewalks where people could bike or walk their bikes if they do not feel comfortable riding on the road.

Cyclists must use local roads to travel between the park's units. While these roads do not have dedicated bike lanes, the pavement is wide enough for cyclists to ride single file on the shoulder. Fast traffic may be a concern to some riders, especially between Meriam's Corner and the Concord Museum, although traffic speeds are not as high here as on Route 2A. Bicycle touring could be combined with travel by shuttle if bicycle racks were installed on shuttle vehicles. This would allow visitors to travel between units without riding on the roads or make a one-way bike tour of the park and use the shuttle to return to their car or the train station.

Map 5
Bike Routes To and Through Minute Man NHP
Source: Mass GIS

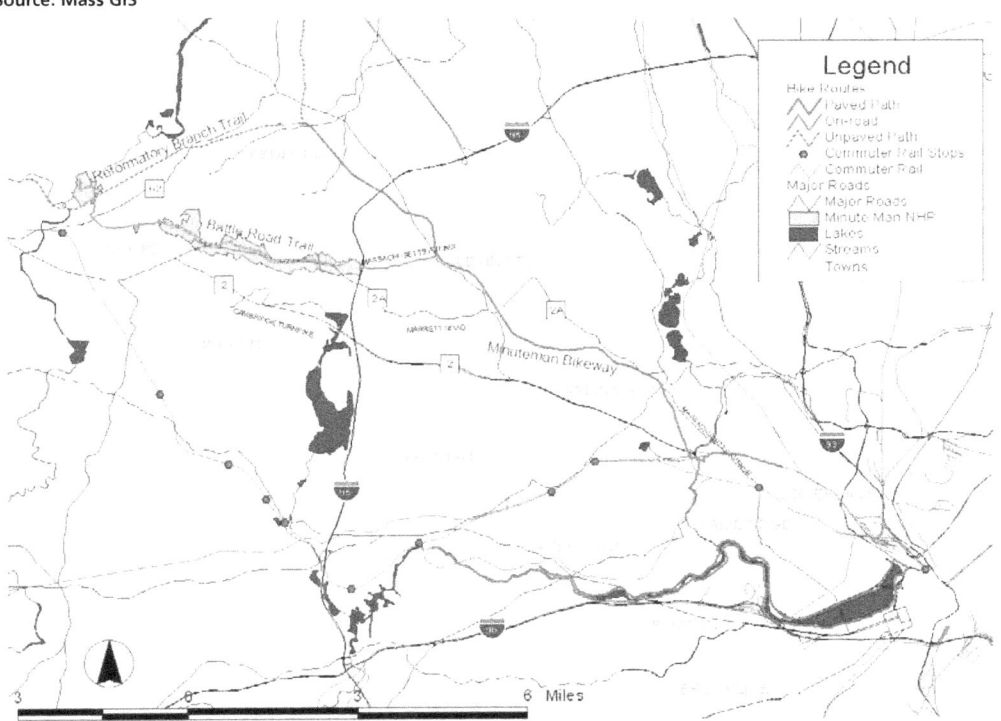

As Access to Park

Bicycle connections to the park are also available. The paved Minuteman Commuter Bikeway runs from the MBTA Alewife Station in Cambridge through Arlington and Lexington to the historic Bedford Depot, just northeast of the park. Exiting the Bikeway in Lexington Center and cycling on public roads, it is approximately 1.5 miles to the beginning of the Battle Road Trail at Fiske Hill. A small sign in Lexington Center directs visitors to travel down Massachusetts Avenue to reach Minute Man NHP. While there is a small hill, traffic along this street is manageable even for novice riders. With a length of 13 miles, this route provides the safest and most direct access from downtown Boston or the city's northwestern suburbs to the park.

Reformatory Branch Trail

The North Bridge is approximately 4.5 miles from the Bedford Depot end of the Bikeway route. Access from this point is more strenuous. The Minuteman Commuter Bikeway Extension/ Reformatory Branch, a dirt path that continues on the right-of-way of the Bikeway provides an off-road option for those with mountain bikes, or one can travel on Route 62. Finding the entrance to the Reformatory Branch from the end of the Bikeway is challenging and it could benefit from better signage. Maps or posted directions are needed by most people to find one's way to the park via Route 62.

Another option is to take the MBTA Commuter Rail to Concord and bike from there to the various park units. In combination with the MBTA Commuter Rail, visiting the park without a car is reasonable for most adults and even some families. Bikes are allowed on MBTA Commuter Rail during non-commute times.[14] Although Concord does not have marked bike lanes and designated routes, most roadways are wide enough to allow cyclists to ride comfortably.

Audience

Biking is an excellent way for park visitors to combine a recreational activity with visiting the park. Families with children are more likely feel comfortable biking on the Battle Road Trail since there is no vehicle traffic.

As discussed above, there are a great number of people who live in Boston and the surrounding cities who do not own a car. Biking to Minute Man NHP may be an attractive option for the car-less who are looking for accessible activities in a more rural setting. Some cyclists may consider extending their recreational rides in the area to the park if they know the infrastructure is available to see the park by bike.

It is important to recognize that while pedestrians and bikers can share right-of-ways, bicycle riders have more of an impact on the surroundings than pedestrians. Bicycles were not a part of the 18th century landscape and may disrupt the ambiance and interpretive experience of other Battle Road Trail users.

Timing

At a conservative 10 miles per hour for off-road biking and 12 miles per hour on-road, bicycling is much faster than walking and requires less effort, which means that trips one would not consider walking are easily made by bike. It is estimated that travel within the park by bike takes approximately two to three times as long as driving, but three to four times less than walking.

The following table provides estimates of cycling travel times. These times do not include stops for interpretation.

Table 2
Bicycling Distance and Times Between Sites

Segment	Distance	Estimated Time
Concord Depot to North Bridge	1.3 miles	7 minutes
Concord Center to The Wayside	0.9 miles	5 minutes
Wayside to Meriam's Corner	0.5 miles	3 minutes
Meriam's Corner to Hartwell Tavern (via Battle Road Trail)	2.8 miles	17 minutes
Hartwell Tavern to Minute Man Visitor Center (via Battle Road Trail)	1.8 miles	11 minutes
Minute Man Visitor Center to Fiske Hill (via Battle Road Trail)	0.9 miles	5 minutes
Boston to Fiske Hill	13.0 miles	65 minutes
Boston to North Bridge	20.6 miles	105 minutes

---

[14] The MBTA schedule (available online at www.mbta.com and at MBTA stations) highlights when bikes are prohibited.

A 40-mile round trip from Boston through the park takes approximately 3.5 hours. Riding through the park starting from the Concord Depot can be completed in 1.5 hours. If the park develops a shuttle service that includes bike racks on the vehicles, traveling one direction by bicycle and then returning to one's starting point by shuttle could shorten trips.

Interpretation

Passive interpretative displays for walkers are also appropriate for bikers on off-road paths such as the Battle Road Trail, as it is easy for a biker to stop to read interpretive information. Personal audio interpretation options such as cell phones are more difficult to incorporate into a bicycle visit to the park unless there are clear points at which cyclists can stop to listen before continuing. As discussed above, group bike tours can be provided in the park and surrounding communities.

Infrastructure

Bikeable routes

As described earlier, there is a good network of bikeable routes to and through the park. The condition of these bikeways is important for providing a safe and satisfying ride. Some portions of the Battle Road Trail can become sandy, which can cause bikes to fishtail or slide out of control, especially for people using thin-tired road bikes. The park's goal is to always maintain the trail with a hard, universally accessible surface. Additional maintenance will be required in order to keep the trail fully accessible.

Route 2A and Route 62 from Bedford provide alternatives to off-road paths, but have high vehicle speeds and unpaved shoulders. Adding bike lanes or paved shoulders can make these on-road alternatives safer.

In and around Concord Town Center and between Lexington Center and Minute Man NHP, roads should be marked to alert drivers to share the road with cyclists. In areas where the right-of-way is wide enough, painting designated bike lanes identifies safer areas for cyclists.

The park has noted opposition to striping bike lanes or posting bike route signs within the park because of a concern for disrupting the historic aesthetic.

In addition to safe bike routes, visitors need bicycles. Rental bikes can be made available at the park to encourage visitors who did not bring their own bicycles, to tour the park in this manner. The park can purchase bikes for use or can work with a concessionaire to rent bikes at the park.

Signage and Interpretation

Bicycle Rack at Hartwell Tavern

Safe, bikeable routes to the park and between different park units need to be publicized with both on-route signs and maps. Locations that are important to link include the Minuteman Bikeway in Lexington Center, the end of the Bikeway in Bedford, Concord Depot, Concord Town Center; the North Bridge, the Wayside, Meriam's Corner, Fiske Hill, and other sites within the Battle Road Unit. It is not believed that additional interpretive infrastructure is needed for bicycle visitors.

Visitor Amenities

Existing visitor amenities such as restrooms and picnic areas are beneficial to cyclists. The park currently has bike racks located at the Minute Man Visitor Center, the North Bridge Visitor Center and Hartwell Tavern. Bike racks are needed at the North Bridge and at The Wayside, so visitors can secure their bikes while exploring these areas by foot.

Costs

Capital costs

In general the cost of encouraging biking at Minute Man is relatively small. Providing directional signage, bike racks, and "Share the Road" markings requires relatively small capital outlays. Adding bike lanes to public roads is more expensive, long-term option, especially if additional right-of-way is needed. Again, consideration of the historic importance of this area would need to be considered in developing on-road infrastructure.

Depending on the current condition of park buildings, facilities for bike rentals could readily be accommodated in an existing structure.

Operating Costs

Guided tours and pathway maintenance constitute the two major ongoing costs. The level of ongoing maintenance depends on the severity of the weather and adequate operating funds. Bike tours were not provided during the 2004 season due to staffing limitations.

Pricing

Charging a fee for self-guided bicycle trips at Minute Man NHP would not be practical. Other services, however, can generate revenue. Organized tours of the park and beyond can require a fee, depending on the length and amenities provided (bicycle rentals, lunch). Daily bike rentals in Boston cost an average of $20-$30, with half-day rentals slightly less expensive.

Partners/Connectivity

Local bicycle advocacy groups such as the Massachusetts Bicycle Coalition (MassBike), Charles River Wheelmen, and Lexington Bicycle Advisory Committee are good potential partners for developing programs, supporting additional infrastructure and publicizing bicycle use in the park. Minute Man NHP needs to work with local jurisdictions to add signage or change the roadway design beyond the park boundaries.

The Bikeway Source at Bedford Depot rents bicycles and can be a partner in encouraging bicycle touring of Minute Man NHP by providing information about bicycling in the park. The park would need to develop a concessionaire agreement via public competition to set up a rental facility within the park.

In addition to park-run bicycle tours, commercial tours can be provided that include additional local or revolutionary sites outside the park. Two commercial vendors were found to advertise such a service.[15]

ATS Benefits

Traffic and Parking Congestion

Unlike walking, bicycling can be a primary transportation mode for travel to the park. In-park bicycling can be paired with bicycling to the park or with use of the MBTA Commuter Rail to provide access to the park, removing vehicles from the park roads and parking lots and reducing vehicle emissions.

Visitor Experience

While not a traditional 18th century mode of transport, bicycling allows visitors to become more immersed in the environment. Since bikes can be used within the park, visitors do not need to visit a site and then return to their cars; they can just continue on to the next site. Bikes also enable

---

[15] The Bicycle Tour Company (www.bicycletours.com), Boston Bike Tours (www.bostonbiketours.com)

visitors to maintain their own speeds and schedules, unlike a tour or shuttle where visitors are locked into a more rigid itinerary.

Park Resources

Biking on unpaved trails such as the Battle Road Trail causes more trail degradation than walking but provides many benefits over driving. Bike parking takes up much less space and is more environmentally supportive than paved parking lots. It can also absorb additional visitation without additional infrastructure. Bikes are also quieter than automobiles and do not produce emissions.

Economic Development

Improvements to bicycle infrastructure in adjacent town centers can provide many benefits to the city, especially for local residents. Adjacent towns frequently have problems with parking and traffic congestion in the downtowns. Locals can be encouraged to bike into town if routes and signage are marked to make them feel more comfortable biking on city roads. This increases the capacity of the town center and reduces the frustrations of being stuck in traffic or circling for parking.

Since biking can be done according to visitors' own schedules, they may be more willing to spend time and money downtown without having to worry about when the next tour or shuttle bus will arrive. Local bike shops also benefit from increased patronage, especially if rentals are available.

Safety

Use of the Battle Road Trail removes park visitors on bikes from Route 2A, reducing the opportunity of vehicle collisions. Higher levels of bicycling throughout the park and in adjacent communities may provide a small level of "traffic calming," as proper signage and previous experiences with bikers slows down drivers and makes them more cognizant of their surroundings. Conversely, on-road bicycling along Route 2A and Route 62 may be hazardous since there are no shoulders and traffic speeds can be quite high. Increased bike use on the Battle Road Trail can lead to an increase in bike-pedestrian conflicts.

Additional Evaluation Needed

Current use of the Battle Road Trail should be monitored for the number of cyclists using the path and how they cycle along the path (speed, physical comfort, number of stops). A more detailed analysis of access roads to the park is needed to determine current bikeability and potential for improvements. Such analysis should focus on roadway width and condition, number of vehicles, and vehicle speeds.

More information on past experiences with bike tours should be gathered, if there is interest in restarting or publicizing these services.

ATP Qualification

Alternative transportation funds can be used for purchasing bicycle racks and for bicycle improvements that provide a connection between other alternative transportation services and the park, such as bike lanes, paths and signage. It is expected that there will be additional support from local jurisdictions for improvements outside of the park. Maintenance of the Battle Road Trail is not eligible for Alternative Transportation Program nor Park Roads and Parkways Program funding. Funds to stabilize and maintain the Battle Road Trail must come from the park operating budget.

Comparison of ATS Options

This table summarizes the relative advantages and disadvantages of each of the ATP options described in this report.

Option	Advantages	Disadvantages
Bus Tours	Excellent interpretive experience Supports visitors with mobility problems Can reduce traffic and parking congestion Supports economic development of local towns Potential partnerships – area towns, Liberty Ride, hotels, chambers of commerce, historic-focused attractions)	Expensive – high capital and operating costs May require user fee Locks visitors into a schedule
Shuttle Bus	Supports visitors with mobility problems Commuter option reduces traffic congestion Can reduce parking congestion Safety – some reduction of short car trips on Route 2A Promotes economic development of local towns Potential partnerships – area towns, LEXPRESS, employment centers, hotels, chambers of commerce, historic-focused attractions)	Expensive – high capital and operating costs May require user fee
Pedestrian Network	Versatile – amenities serve almost all park users Improves visitor access to most areas of park Inexpensive – most of basic elements have low capital cost and no ongoing operational costs Flexible – can be combined with shuttle or other ATS options Potential partnerships – area towns, hiking organizations, local businesses, etc.	Limited application – unrealistic to rely on pedestrian connections between park's units Small audience for trips *to* the park
Bicycle Network	Good combination of visitor convenience and low impact on park Inexpensive – many of basic elements have low capital cost and no ongoing operational costs Potential partnerships – area towns, bike organizations, local businesses, etc.	Improvements to roadways (for bike lanes) are expensive

Next Steps

Based on the information collected for this report and the preliminary findings, there are certain logical next steps to move forward with the development and implementation of additional alternative transportation systems at Minute Man NHP.

Additional Data Collection

NPS staff will need specific data to target its alternative transportation efforts to the needs of the park and its visitors. Empirical observations, visitor surveys, and review of local planning documents can provide the following needed information:

- Visitor use patterns at the park
- Levels of usage (especially Battle Road Trail)
- Length and purposes of trips
- Parking lot capacity by time of day, day of week, and season
- Vehicle speed and volume counts on Route 2A
- Commuter transit patterns
- Visitor interest in each of the specific alternative transportation options
- Willingness to use each of options
- Preferences for locations and routes
- Willingness to pay a fee for options (tour, bus, horse)
- Potential partners' levels of interest and financial participation
- Financial analysis for options with ongoing revenue and operating costs
- Liberty Ride operating costs and ridership
- Areas of conflict between visitor and commuter uses
- Pedestrian and vehicular uses that pose access, enjoyment, and safety concerns
- Bicycle route analysis including on-road conditions
- Information about existing and previous bike tours at the park

Narrow the Options

Based on the information in this report and additional data collection efforts, park staff will be able to identify the alternative transportation option(s) in which there is the most interest and which they deem the most feasible. After this determination, the chosen option(s) should be developed more thoroughly. This process should be integrated into upcoming GMP and corridor management projects. Additional alternative transportation efforts should focus on the data needed to prepare estimates of anticipated usage, financial plans, and projected impacts on the park, in order to develop more detailed proposals for the specific project(s). A visitor survey can provide much of this information.

Conclusion

This document presents an overview of the current transportation environment in the area of Minute Man NHP. Current conditions, including existing transit services and stakeholder attitudes, indicate that additional alternative transportation systems would likely benefit the park. The four options examined in this report (bus tour service, shuttle bus service, pedestrian networks, and bicycle networks) are all viable at Minute Man NHP, although each has its own advantages and disadvantages. The park will need to collect additional data and work with its partners to determine which services are most desirable and how to finance and operate them.

Stakeholder Information

Janel Blood
Executive Director
Concord Chamber of Commerce
100 Main Street, Suite 310-2
Concord, Massachusetts 01742
978.369.3120
admin@concordmachamber.org

William Bunce
General Manager
Sheraton Lexington Inn
727 Marrett Road
Lexington, Massachusetts 02421
781.862.8700
bill.bunce@sheraton.com

Greg Cravedi
Environmental Protection Specialist
Hanscom Air Force Base
Bedford, Massachusetts 01730
781.377.7950

Tom Ennis
Senior Project Manager
Economic Planning & Development
Massachusetts Port Authority
One Harborside Drive, Suite 200S
East Boston, Massachusetts 02128
617.568.3546
tennis@massport.com

Glenn Garber
Director
Lexington Planning Department
1625 Massachusetts Avenue
Lexington, Massachusetts 02420
781.862.0500 extension 246
ggarber@ci.lexington.ma.us

John Ott
Executive Director
National Heritage Museum
33 Marrett Road
Lexington, Massachusetts 02421
781.457.4102
jott@monh.org

Marcia Rasmussen
Director of Planning and Land Management
Elizabeth Hughes
Staff Planner
Concord Department of Planning & Land Management
141 Keyes Road
Concord, Massachusetts 01742
978.318.3290
mrassmussen@concordnet.org

Larry Smith
President
Cranberry Hill Associates. Inc.
Lincoln North
Lincoln, Massachusetts 01773
781.259.4100
lsmith@cranberryhillassoc.com

Masha Taber
Coordinator
Liberty Ride
781.863.5966
mtraber@rcn.com

Mark Whitehead
Town Planner
Town of Lincoln
16 Lincoln Road
Lincoln, Massachusetts 01773
781.259.2684
whiteheadm@lincolntown.org

www.ingramcontent.com/pod-product-compliance
Lightning Source LLC
Chambersburg PA
CBHW081902170526
45167CB00007B/3112